Early Praise for *Hotwire Native for Rails Developers: Build Native Mobile Apps Using Your Server*

Joe teaches Hotwire Native wonderfully from a Rails developer's perspective. He translates ideas you already know from Ruby on Rails into the new mental models you need for iOS and Android development. I highly recommend this book for anyone wanting to build Hotwire Native apps for their Ruby on Rails applications!

➤ **Chris Oliver**
  Founder, GoRails

Joe has long been a leading light in the Hotwire Native and Rails community, sharing blog posts and videos and contributing to the frameworks directly. This book is the culmination of all that work and is immediately the definitive reference for building Hotwire Native apps with Rails.

➤ **Miles Woodroffe**
  CTO, Mindful Chef

This is the missing Hotwire Native manual. Hotwire Native is the fastest, easiest way to deliver a mobile Rails app, and Joe's instruction is clear, focused, and readable. If you're a Rails developer interested in mobile apps, this book is for you.

➤ **David L. Bean**
  Startup CTO and Faculty, University of Utah Kahlert School of Computing

Reading this book is like listening to a knowledgeable and enthusiastic teacher. That enthusiasm is infectious, and it enhances learning by building and maintaining interest in the topic. This is especially noticeable when reading about the ways that Hotwire Native makes life easier as a developer.

➤ **André Brown**
  Rails Developer

Hotwire Native empowers small teams to rapidly deploy across multiple platforms with very little native code. Joe's work throughout the years sets a great example that has personally inspired me to pursue Hotwire Native development. This book is the perfect blueprint to help you deploy your Hotwire Native-enabled web app straight to the Apple and Google app stores.

➤ **William Kennedy**
  Web Developer, williamkennedy.ninja

Hotwire Native for Rails Developers

Build Native Mobile Apps Using Your Server

Joe Masilotti

The Pragmatic Bookshelf

Dallas, Texas

Pragmatic
Bookshelf

See our complete catalog of hands-on, practical,
and Pragmatic content for software developers:
https://pragprog.com

Sales, volume licensing, and support:
support@pragprog.com

Derivative works, AI training and testing,
international translations, and other rights:
rights@pragprog.com

The team that produced this book includes:

Publisher:	Dave Thomas
COO:	Janet Furlow
Executive Editor:	Susannah Davidson
Series Editor:	Noel Rappin
Development Editor:	Nicole Taché
Copy Editor:	Corina Lebegioara
Indexing:	Potomac Indexing, LLC
Layout:	Gilson Graphics

ISBN-13: 979-8-88865-151-3
Book version: P1.0—August 2025

Contents

Foreword

The mission of Ruby on Rails has always been to enable the single developer to do it all: build a front-end, build a back-end, build everything needed to take a great web application from HELLO WORLD to launch and beyond. Over the past two decades, countless developers have done just that, and some of the most important web apps on the Internet are powered by Rails because of this.

But building a business on the Internet today now often requires more than just building for a generic browser. In many industries, native applications for iOS and Android have become table stakes. And the work required to build these using the official toolkits often turns out to be orders of magnitude more than the web app. In many cases, this means it's simply unrealistic for a single developer to do it all.

Hotwire Native changes that for Rails developers. By using the power of Hotwire, you no longer have to replace the entire web app, and constantly keep it in sync, with a duplicated set of native applications for the two dominant platforms. Instead, you can let that wonderful web app be the basis for everything, wrap it in a great, native shell for navigation, and only build native interactions where it's really needed.

That's what we do at 37signals for both Basecamp and HEY, our project management and email+calendar systems. The vast majority of the screens in these applications are the same as they are for the web app version, only with custom CSS to tweak the presentation for the smaller screen. This has allowed us to run two massive applications, with tens of thousands of paying customers and millions of total users, with a tiny team. It has also allowed us to update the applications rapidly and outside the onerous app store review process for the majority of new features and fixes we ship.

It's from this work that Hotwire Native has been extracted. This isn't a science or a hobby project. Hotwire Native is the foundation for real-life commercial apps that bring in millions of dollars every month. It's what allows us to ship new major features every six weeks, often without involving our native developers at all, when the web is enough. And when the interaction calls for it, we can always level it up to native fidelity at a later date. The gears of coordination don't have to grind.

You can learn how to do this, too. You can learn how to become capable, as a single developer or as part of a team, of building and maintaining fantastic hybrid applications for iOS and Android, while continuing to lean on the ease of development that Ruby on Rails has always been known for. This book will teach you how. Joe Masilotti will teach you how. He's the foremost expert outside of 37signals on Hotwire Native, so you couldn't be in better hands.

Now build something awesome and ship it!

— David Heinemeier Hansson

Acknowledgments

First, I want to thank Eric Stephens, who introduced me to Hotwire Native back in 2016 when it was called Turbolinks Native. That moment changed the trajectory of my career. Without him taking a big bet on a brand-new, technically unreleased framework, I might never have gotten interested in building hybrid mobile apps.

I'm grateful to the amazing team at PragProg for their constant support and encouragement throughout this journey—especially my editor, Nicole Taché, who guided this book from the first page to the last. Thanks also to Dave Thomas, Margaret Eldridge, Juliet Thomas, and Susannah Davidson for their invaluable contributions behind the scenes, making this book a reality.

Thank you to Denis Švara, Fernando Olivares, Zoë Smith, and the rest of the mobile team at 37signals for building Hotwire Native and cheering me on. And a special shout-out to Jay Ohms, who was always quick to answer my (many, many) questions while I was writing this book.

I'm so thankful to the reviewers, especially those who took the time to read messy first drafts in Notion. Your feedback means the world to me: Miles Woodroffe, William Kennedy, Robbie Clutton, Adam Pallozzi, Chris Oliver, David L. Bean, Corinn Pope, John Paul Ashenfelter, André Brown, and Michael Fazio. And to anyone who replied to an email or reached out on social media, you've given me the energy to keep going.

And to my family—Adrienne, Duke, and Miles. Thank you for your never-ending love, patience, and support. This book wouldn't exist without you.

Finally, thank *you* for picking up this book and giving Hotwire Native a shot. You're the reason I write.

Preface

Welcome to *Hotwire Native for Rails Developers*!

I'm Joe Masilotti, the Hotwire Native guy.[1] I help Ruby on Rails developers build server-powered iOS and Android apps with Hotwire Native.

I became the Hotwire Native guy in 2016 when I was tasked with launching a 100+ screen Rails app to the App Store and Google Play. With the help of Hotwire Native, I was able to do this in a few months—*as the only developer on the team*. This would have taken me *years* if I'd gone fully native!

My world changed the day those apps went live in the app stores. And since then I've been *all in* on Hotwire Native.

Over the years, I've learned a lot about Hotwire Native. I know where it shines and where it falls short. And I'm excited to share everything I know with you.

The Problem with Native Apps

Building fully native iOS and Android apps is a *lot* of work. They are expensive to build and even more expensive to maintain. Developers have to build every screen three times: once for the web, once for iOS, and once for Android. For small teams, this just isn't viable.

Every new feature or bug fix release also requires a review by the app store teams. At best, this can delay a mission-critical bug fix for 24 hours. But it's not unheard of for reviews to take up to a week or more.

There's also the complexity of maintaining separate codebases. Fully native apps require all of your business logic to be built in Ruby, Swift, *and* Kotlin. Re-implementing the same thing three times almost guarantees inconsistencies.

So, if you're a Rails developer who wants to build mobile apps for both iOS and Android, what are you to do?

---

1. https://masilotti.com

The Hybrid Solution

Enter Hotwire Native, a framework that builds hybrid mobile apps for iOS and Android. It renders HTML from your Rails server in an embedded web view, packaged inside a native app. You build your screens once, in HTML, and then deploy them across the web, iOS, and Android *simultaneously*. Deploy to your server and you're done. No repackaging apps or resubmitting to app stores.

And Hotwire Native maximizes your skills by giving you more time to do what you do best—*writing Ruby code*. Most of your logic will remain on the server, with the apps acting as thin clients to your HTML.

While fully native apps are expensive to build and maintain, Hotwire Native apps are not. After an initial upfront cost, it's possible to not touch the native code again for years. I had the same version of a Hotwire Native app in the App Store for almost *five years*, all while receiving weekly feature updates and bug fixes via changes to the Rails codebase.

Finally, when a web experience isn't cutting it, you can drop down to Swift or Kotlin. These components and screens can be upgraded to native on a case-by-case basis. It's not all or nothing. This means you can tackle that new feature when the team is ready, without having to block the launch of your initial release.

No other framework does this. *Hotwire Native gives Rails developers super-powers.*

Prerequisites

This book assumes you have a decent understanding of building applications with Ruby on Rails and Hotwire. If you can create a basic CRUD app and add a few Stimulus controllers, you'll be fine. No Swift or Kotlin experience is necessary. I recommend *Agile Web Development with Rails 8*[2] and *Modern Front-End Development for Rails*[3] if you'd like to brush up on your Rails skills.

To get the most out of this book, I recommend building the apps as you follow along. To do so, you'll need to run a Rails server, Xcode, and Android Studio.

---

2. https://pragprog.com/titles/rails8/agile-web-development-with-rails-8/
3. https://pragprog.com/titles/nrclient2/modern-front-end-development-for-rails-second-edition/

To run the Rails app, you'll need to have Ruby 3.4.2 and SQLite[4] installed. And you'll need Xcode[5] 16 and Android Studio[6] Meerkat or later on macOS to build the mobile apps.

How This Book Is Structured

This book walks you through building a Hotwire Native app on iOS and Android. We'll start with an existing Rails codebase and quickly dive into creating new Xcode and Android Studio projects for the apps.

You can find the reference code on the book's website.[7] There you'll also find a link to a forum with any errors, typos, or suggestions.

You'll build a small hiking tracker, which will provide a quick way to log some notes and a photo from your strolls through nature. Most of the content will be rendered from the server. We'll also progressively enhance screens to add native functionality, like maps.

Each chapter builds a new feature into the apps by introducing a new Hotwire Native concept. Most follow the same cadence: we'll first cover the Rails code, then iOS, and finally Android. If you're only interested in building for one platform, then feel free to skip the other and come back to it later.

Need Help?

If you have any questions or need help, don't hesitate to reach out. You can find me in my Discord server[8] or send me an email.[9] I'd love to hear from you.

---

4.   https://www.sqlite.org
5.   https://developer.apple.com/xcode/
6.   https://developer.android.com/studio
7.   https://pragprog.com/titles/jmnative/hotwire-native-for-rails-developers/
8.   https://masilotti.com/discord
9.   joe@masilotti.com

Build Your First Hotwire Native Apps

In this first chapter, we're going to dive right in and build a Hotwire Native app on iOS and Android from scratch.

The hiking journal apps you'll build in this book are powered by a small Rails server with some basic functionality built in. Hotwire Native, the framework we'll use to build the apps, renders HTML from your Rails server in an embedded web view, packaged inside a native app.

To run the Rails app, make sure you have Ruby 3.4.2 and SQLite[1] installed. And, if you haven't already, download and install Xcode[2] 16 and Android Studio[3] Meerkat or later, now. They're both pretty heavy IDEs and can take a while to download.

The reference code[4] that comes with this book has a bunch of subdirectories. Each corresponds to a different step when building the apps. Start with the code in ch01_00, meaning "chapter one checkpoint zero." Each time a code change is introduced in the book, it will increment the second number: ch01_01, ch01_02, ch01_03, and so on. Each chapter will increment the first number: ch01_01, ch02_01, ch03_01, and so on. Feel free to use these to double-check your work or as a checkpoint if you jump ahead to a later chapter.

Now, copy the code to your machine and navigate to the ch01_00 directory. Create and seed the database by switching to the rails directory and running bin/setup on the command line.

---

1. https://www.sqlite.org
2. https://developer.apple.com/xcode/
3. https://developer.android.com/studio
4. https://media.pragprog.com/titles/jmnative/code/jmnative-code.zip

ActiveRecord::AssociationTypeMismatch

If running bin/setup raises an ActiveRecord::AssociationTypeMismatch exception, try running the seeds manually via bin/rails db:seed. There's an inconsistency with SQLite https://github.com/rails/rails/issues/53832 that's currently being addressed.

Then, start the server via bin/dev and visit http://localhost:3000 to check out what we're working with. The app is a basic CRUD application to keep track of our nature hikes with some basic styling from Bootstrap.[5] Users can create, read, update, and delete entries, as well as upload an image from their trek.

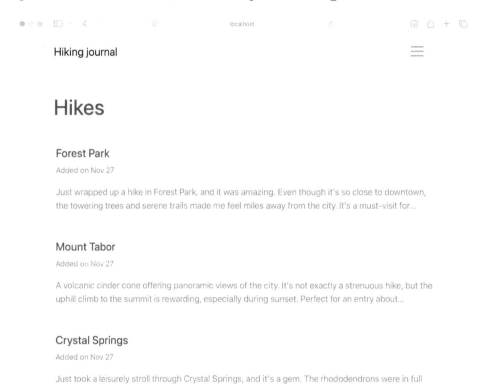

With our server running, let's create a basic iOS app with Hotwire Native.

---

5. https://getbootstrap.com

Build a Hotwire Native iOS App

To build your first Hotwire Native app on iOS, you'll follow three steps: create a new Xcode project, add the Hotwire Native package, and configure the app to get it running. Are you ready to write your first line of Swift?

Create a New Xcode Project

Start by creating a new project by opening Xcode and clicking Create New Project... in the welcome window. Or, click File → New → New Project....

Select iOS at the top and then App from the Application section. Click Next.

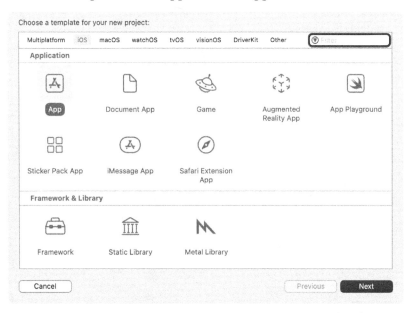

Enter "HikingJournal" (no spaces) for the Product Name. Make sure Interface is set to Storyboard, Language to Swift, and Testing System to None.

Finally, fill in the Organization Identifier. The App Store uses this to uniquely identify apps; it will never be shown to users. I like to use reverse domain name notation,[6] which converts my company website masilotti.com to an Organization Identifier of com.masilotti.

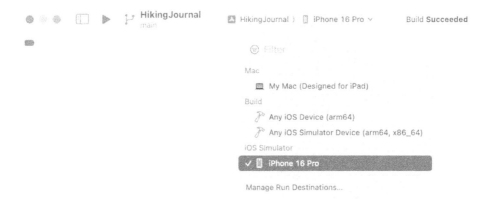

Click Next and choose a location on your machine to store the project. I recommend a directory next to the Rails code named ios. Finally, click Create.

Ensure a simulator is selected as the run destination at the top of Xcode to the right of HikingJournal. If your iPhone is plugged in or nearby, you might see that selected instead.

---

6. https://en.wikipedia.org/wiki/Reverse_domain_name_notation

Click Product → Run or press ⌘ R to build and run your app. If all went well, you should see a very exciting, completely blank, white screen in the simulator!

As exciting as launching an app in the simulator may be, I'd like the app to actually do something useful. Up next, you'll add the Hotwire Native package to start filling that white space with content from the Rails app.

Add the Hotwire Native Package

Hotwire Native is added to the app as a Swift package. Swift packages are like Ruby gems, allowing you to use third-party code in your project.

Add the Hotwire Native package by clicking File → Add Package Dependencies... in Xcode. An interface to the Swift Package Manager will appear, Swift's equivalent to Bundler.

Enter the following hotwire-native-ios package URL in the search box at the upper right (as seen in the following screen). Change the Dependency Rule to Up to Next *Minor* Version and enter 1.2.0 for the version number. Click Add Package.

```
https://github.com/hotwired/hotwire-native-ios
```

On the next screen, make sure HikingJournal is selected under Add to Target. Then click Add Package again to add it to the project.

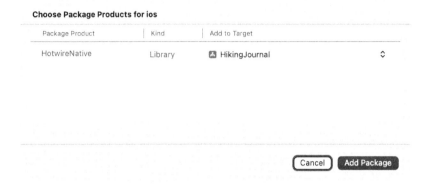

Hotwire Native and Future Updates

Hotwire Native is introducing breaking changes in *minor* version updates, for example, from v1.2 to v1.3. We selected "Up to Next Minor Version" in the Swift Package Manager dialog because this approach is slightly different than the official semantic versioning[7] guidelines.

Xcode will add a new section to your *Project Navigator*, the currently open navigator on the left, titled Package Dependencies. The Hotwire package will appear beneath that. We're free to dig into the code here, just as if we typed bundle open in a Rails app.

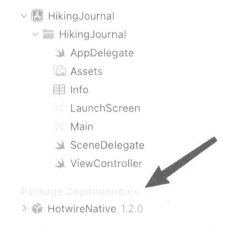

The Hotwire Native package is now integrated. So, let's get something on the screen!

---

7.   https://semver.org

Get the iOS App Running

Double-click SceneDelegate from the Project Navigator to open this file in the *editor area* in the center of the screen. This pane is where you'll write Swift code and where you'll spend most of your time in Xcode.

Apple provides a bunch of boilerplate code with new projects. But it assumes you're building a more traditional native app, not a hybrid one. So, for the Hotwire Native developer, this boilerplate code isn't that useful. Start by deleting the contents of the file. Yep, everything! You'll build up what you need, and only what you need, one line at a time.

A heads-up that I'll refer to files without their extension moving forward, for example, SceneDelegate.swift. But Xcode won't show the extension in the Project Navigator until you edit the filename.

Import Frameworks

Swift files have access to the Swift standard library and all code in the current package, your Xcode project. If you're referencing other code, then it needs to be imported. SceneDelegate uses the UIKit framework for building UI elements and the Hotwire framework for interacting with our Rails server. Import these frameworks at the top of SceneDelegete:

ch01_01/ios/HikingJournal/SceneDelegate.swift
```
import HotwireNative
import UIKit
```

Add a baseURL Variable

Then declare a variable that points to the Rails server via let, making it a *constant*. Swift encourages immutability whenever possible. Knowing that a variable can never change often makes it easier to understand how data will flow through the code in your app.

ch01_02/ios/HikingJournal/SceneDelegate.swift
```
import HotwireNative
import UIKit

➤ let baseURL = URL(string: "http://localhost:3000")!
```

There's something to notice with the baseURL variable: there's an exclamation point at the end of the URL initializer. This is because URL(string:) returns an *optional* value. Optional variables behave like Ruby ones—they can also be nil. Non-optional variables in Swift must *always* contain a value and can never be nil.

For baseURL, the compiler can't guarantee the arbitrary string we pass in is a valid URL, so the check happens at runtime. If it's invalid, it returns nil. Adding an exclamation point tells the compiler to *force unwrap* the optional variable, returning a non-optional URL class.

Force Unwrapping Optionals

A heads-up that force unwrapping a nil value will crash your app! This should only be done when you're 100% confident there won't be a nil value present. We'll touch on safer operations to access potentially nil values later in the book.

Create the SceneDelegate Class

Like Ruby, Swift files often contain a single class or concept named after the filename. After the baseURL variable, create a new class with the class keyword and call it SceneDelegate:

ch01_03/ios/HikingJournal/SceneDelegate.swift
```
import HotwireNative
import UIKit

let baseURL = URL(string: "http://localhost:3000")!

class SceneDelegate {
}
```

The "delegate" suffix refers to the *delegate* design pattern in iOS. This provides a way for objects to act on behalf of others to handle specific events, like when the app launches or a push notification is received. Delegates are similar to ActiveRecord callbacks like before_validation and after_save.

Add the window and navigator Properties

Inside the SceneDelegate class, add a property named window. This holds the actual interface that the user sees:

ch01_04/ios/HikingJournal/SceneDelegate.swift
```
import HotwireNative
import UIKit

let baseURL = URL(string: "http://localhost:3000")!

class SceneDelegate {
    var window: UIWindow?
}
```

Unlike Ruby, variables in Swift must be explicitly typed. The question mark at the end of the UIWindow type makes this property optional. window needs to be optional because it's assigned after SceneDelegate is instantiated. But you won't ever assign anything to the window directly, iOS takes care of that when the app launches.

After the window, create a Navigator property. Part of Hotwire Native, this property abstracts the navigation between web screens and acts as our main interface to the framework. We configure it with an arbitrary name, "main". A unique name is required when using multiple Navigator instances, like when we get to multiple tabs in Chapter 4, Add a Native Tab Bar, on page 61. startLocation is set to the page we want to load when the app is launched, /hikes.

ch01_05/ios/HikingJournal/SceneDelegate.swift
```
import HotwireNative
import UIKit

let baseURL = URL(string: "http://localhost:3000")!

class SceneDelegate {
    var window: UIWindow?

    private let navigator = Navigator(configuration: .init(
        name: "main",
        startLocation: baseURL.appending(path: "hikes")
    ))
}
```

The navigator is an implementation detail of SceneDelegate. No one else needs to know about it, so we can make it private. It's also declared with let, making it a constant. This means that, unlike our window property declared with var from the previous example, the value of navigator can never be changed.

Inherit and Implement

When the app launches, iOS calls a special function. SceneDelegate needs to implement this for our app to launch correctly. To make this happen, add a colon after SceneDelegate and add the UIResponder class and UIWindowSceneDelegate protocol:

ch01_06/ios/HikingJournal/SceneDelegate.swift
```
import HotwireNative
import UIKit

let baseURL = URL(string: "http://localhost:3000")!

class SceneDelegate: UIResponder, UIWindowSceneDelegate {
    var window: UIWindow?

    private let navigator = Navigator(configuration: .init(
        name: "main",
        startLocation: baseURL.appending(path: "hikes")
    ))
}
```

Protocols in Swift are most similar to abstract classes in Rails. On their own, they only contain property and function definitions, no implementation.

After our navigator property, add the function required for the app to launch:

ch01_07/ios/HikingJournal/SceneDelegate.swift
```
import HotwireNative
import UIKit

let baseURL = URL(string: "http://localhost:3000")!

class SceneDelegate: UIResponder, UIWindowSceneDelegate {
    var window: UIWindow?

    private let navigator = Navigator(configuration: .init(
        name: "main",
        startLocation: baseURL.appending(path: "hikes")
    ))

    func scene(
        _ scene: UIScene,
        willConnectTo session: UISceneSession,
        options connectionOptions: UIScene.ConnectionOptions
    ) {
    }
}
```

The function being called is our trigger to start rendering some content.

Functions in Swift

Functions in Swift look pretty different than methods in Ruby. Like properties of a class, each parameter in Swift must also have a type.

The following function takes two parameters of type Int and returns another Int:

```
func add(x: Int, y: Int) -> Int {
    x + y
}
add(x: 1, y: 2) // Returns 3
```

We call functions in Swift just like we call Ruby methods, with named parameters. We can *omit* a parameter from the call site by using an underscore:

```
func add(_ x: Int, _ y: Int) -> Int {
    x + y
}
add(1, 2) // Returns 3
```

Or we can *rename* a parameter for the implementation:

```
func add(first x: Int, second y: Int) -> Int {
    x + y
}
```

```
add(first: 1, second: 2) // Returns 3
```

Functions are referenced by their call site parameters without types. The three functions you just saw would be referenced in documentation as add(x:y:), add(_:_:) and add(first:second:).

Set a Root View Controller

For iOS to actually render anything, we need to attach a *view controller* to the main window. View controllers, subclasses of UIViewController, are the building blocks of iOS applications. They are kind of like combining a Rails controller and a Rails view into one, as view controllers manage the state of the UI and are responsible for rendering it. With a few exceptions, individual screens and view controllers share a 1:1 relationship.

Grab the rootViewController from Navigator and assign it to the window's root view controller property:

ch01_08/ios/HikingJournal/SceneDelegate.swift
```
import HotwireNative
import UIKit

let baseURL = URL(string: "http://localhost:3000")!

class SceneDelegate: UIResponder, UIWindowSceneDelegate {
    // ...

    func scene(
        _ scene: UIScene,
        willConnectTo session: UISceneSession,
        options connectionOptions: UIScene.ConnectionOptions
    ) {
        window?.rootViewController = navigator.rootViewController
    }
}
```

The question mark after window is similar to the Safe Navigation Operator in Ruby (&.). We can chain calls with the question mark to safely work with optionals. If the underlying value is nil, then nothing happens—just like in Ruby.

When the app launches, it will now render the navigator's screen hierarchy.

Initiate the Visit

Next, tell Navigator to visit the hikes index page by calling start().

ch01_09/ios/HikingJournal/SceneDelegate.swift

```swift
import HotwireNative
import UIKit

let baseURL = URL(string: "http://localhost:3000")!

class SceneDelegate: UIResponder, UIWindowSceneDelegate {
    // ...

    func scene(
        _ scene: UIScene,
        willConnectTo session: UISceneSession,
        options connectionOptions: UIScene.ConnectionOptions
    ) {
        window?.rootViewController = navigator.rootViewController
        navigator.start()
    }
}
```

Click Product → Run or press ⌘ R to build and run the app. The homepage of the Rails app will appear in the simulator.

Sign in by opening the hamburger menu at the top of the screen and tapping Sign in. The form is populated with credentials for the demo account, so just tap the submit button to authenticate. Once signed in, add a hike via the "Add a hike" button at the bottom of the screen.

We didn't build *any* of this functionality into the iOS app. We get it all for free from Hotwire Native, rendering our Rails HTML content. Amazing!

You Just Built an iOS App!

Congratulations! You've officially built your first Hotwire Native app on iOS. You learned how to create a new Xcode project, build a basic iOS app, and navigate to a page with Navigator. You even picked up some Swift along the way, like optionals, unwrapping, and protocols.

The app is off to a great start, but there are a few rough edges, especially around viewing and submitting the forms to add and update hikes. We'll explore different ways of handling forms with *modals* in Chapter 3, Navigate Gracefully with Path Configuration, on page 47.

But for now, let's switch gears to Android. Feel free to skip this part if you only want to focus on iOS. You can always come back later for the Android details.

Build a Hotwire Native Android App

Start by creating a new project by opening Android Studio and clicking New Project in the welcome window. Or, click File → New → New Project....

Select the Phone and Tablet category from the left and then the Empty *Views* Activity template (not Empty Activity at the top). Click Next.

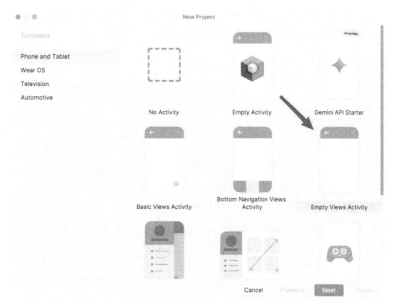

Enter "Hiking Journal" for the Name and "com.masilotti.hikingjournal" for the Package name. Like the organization identifier on iOS, Google Play uses the package name to uniquely identify apps in the store. Choose a save location on your machine—I recommend a directory next to the Rails code named android. Also, make sure Kotlin is selected for the Language and API 28 (or higher) is selected for the Minimum SDK.

Empty Views Activity

Creates a new empty activity

Name	HikingJournal
Package name	com.masilotti.hikingjournal
Save location	/Users/joemasilotti/workspace/book/code/android
Language	Kotlin
Minimum SDK	API 28 ("Pie"; Android 9.0)
	ⓘ Your app will run on approximately **93.4%** of devices. Help me choose
Build configuration language	Kotlin DSL (build.gradle.kts) [Recommended]

At the time of publication, Android 9 (API 28) runs on approximately 93.4% of devices, as seen in the previous screenshot. That's the minimum requirement for Hotwire Native, so I recommend using that unless you need specific features from a more recent release.

Click Finish to create the app.

When Android Studio finishes downloading and configuring the project, make sure that the Android view is selected from the dropdown in the upper left as shown in the first screenshot on page 15. If you see Project, click it and change it to Android.

Before we run the app, we need to confirm two settings. Depending on which version of Android Studio you're running, your project might be configured to use older versions of Android and/or Kotlin.

From the left pane, expand the chevron next to Gradle Scripts and double-click the *second* build.gradle.kts (the *app* one, not the project) to open it, as shown in the second screenshot on page 15.

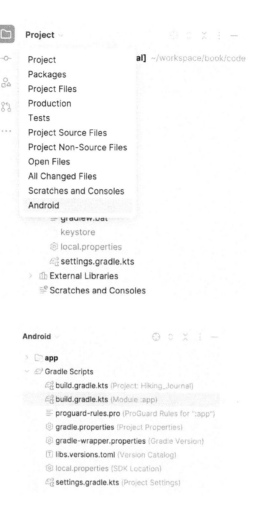

Gradle[8] is similar to Bundler in Ruby but is much more powerful. It not only manages dependencies like a Gemfile but also handles tasks like compiling your app, packaging resources, running tests, and creating different build versions (for example, debug vs. release).

In this file, make sure that compileSdk and targetSdk are set to version 35. Without this, your app might fail to build.

ch01_11/android/app/build.gradle.kts
```
plugins {
    alias(libs.plugins.android.application)
    alias(libs.plugins.kotlin.android)
}
```

---

8.   https://developer.android.com/build

```
android {
    namespace = "com.masilotti.hikingjournal"
    compileSdk = 35

    defaultConfig {
        applicationId = "com.masilotti.hikingjournal"
        minSdk = 28
        targetSdk = 35
        versionCode = 1
        versionName = "1.0"

        testInstrumentationRunner = "androidx.test.runner.AndroidJUnitRunner"
    }

    // ...
}
```

Then, open libs.versions.toml and make sure Kotlin is set to 2.0.0 or later.

ch01_11/android/gradle/libs.versions.toml
```
[versions]
agp = "8.9.2"
kotlin = "2.1.0"
coreKtx = "1.16.0"
junit = "4.13.2"
junitVersion = "1.2.1"
espressoCore = "3.6.1"
appcompat = "1.7.0"
material = "1.12.0"
activity = "1.10.1"
constraintlayout = "2.2.1"

# ...
```

If you changed anything, then Android Studio will complain that Gradle files have changed and the project needs to be synchronized. Resolve this by clicking the Sync Now button in the yellow bar at the top of the screen.

When synced, run the app by clicking the green arrow at the top of the screen or by clicking Run → Run 'app'. Your first Android app. Nice work!

Before we add the Hotwire Native dependency, I want to share two personal IDE preferences I configure in Android Studio: light mode and detached emulators. Feel free to skip ahead if you aren't interested in either of these.

Configure Android Studio (Optional)

Enable light mode by clicking Android Studio → Settings…. Select Appearance from the Appearance & Behavior category on the left. Then change the Theme option from Dark to Light with Light Header.

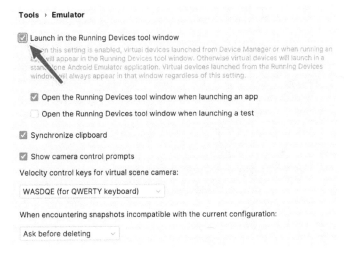

Light mode? From a developer?! I know, silly me, right? But for some reason, I like the way it looks. It also makes the screenshots in this book appear a lot cleaner!

Detaching the Android emulator from Android Studio, my other IDE preference, lets it run in its own window, like the iOS simulator. Search for "emulator" in the Settings search bar, and uncheck "Launch in the Running Devices tool window." Restart Android Studio for this to take effect.

OK, back to Hotwire Native.

Add the Hotwire Native Dependency

Like the Swift package on iOS, Hotwire Native is added to the Android app as a Gradle dependency. Scroll to the bottom of the *app* build.gradle.kts (the *second* one) and add the Hotwire Native dependency to the dependencies section:

ch01_12/android/app/build.gradle.kts

```
// ...

dependencies {
    implementation(libs.androidx.core.ktx)
    implementation(libs.androidx.appcompat)
    implementation(libs.material)
    implementation(libs.androidx.activity)
    implementation(libs.androidx.constraintlayout)
    implementation("dev.hotwire:core:1.2.0")
    implementation("dev.hotwire:navigation-fragments:1.2.0")
    testImplementation(libs.junit)
    androidTestImplementation(libs.androidx.junit)
    androidTestImplementation(libs.androidx.espresso.core)
}
```

Sync Gradle again to make the Hotwire Native library available to your codebase. Like on iOS, the next step is to get the Android app running so we can see our Rails content on the screen.

Gradle Version Catalogs

For this book, we'll set each dependency's version number in the same file we declare the dependency. For more complex Android apps, you can set version numbers in lib.versions.toml. The documentation[9] says this:

> Gradle version catalogs enable you to add and maintain dependencies and plugins in a scalable way. Using Gradle version catalogs makes managing dependencies and plugins easier when you have multiple modules. Instead of hardcoding dependency names and versions in individual build files and updating each entry whenever you need to upgrade a dependency, you can create a central version catalog of dependencies that various modules can reference in a type-safe way with Android Studio assistance.

This is handy for when the next version of Hotwire Native is released—you'd only have to change a single line in the [versions] section to update both dependencies.

---

9.   https://developer.android.com/build/migrate-to-catalogs

Get the Android App Running

Rendering web content on a mobile app requires a compatible *fragment* with an embedded web view. Fragments in Android are similar to view controllers in iOS: they manage the logic, interaction, and sometimes layout of content. Fragments usually map 1:1 with screens. Hotwire Native provides a fragment with everything we need. All we have to do is put it on the screen and configure it.

Update the Layout

From the left panel, expand app, res, and then layout. This directory contains all the view layouts for the app, currently only activity_main.xml. Double-click that file to open it.

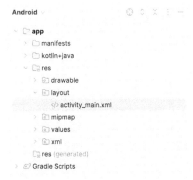

The default view is a visual editor and has a lot going on. I was pretty over-whelmed the first time I saw this! We only need to change a few lines, though, so let's edit the XML directly. Click the Code icon in the upper right, represented by four horizontal lines, to view the underlying XML code.

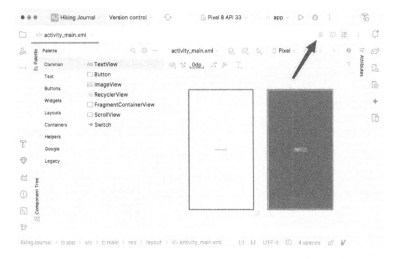

Ah, much better!

This file has two nodes: the outer ConstraintLayout wraps an inner TextView. See the "Hello World!" string? That's where that text came from when you first launched the app.

We want to render a FragmentContainerView. This manages the stack of screens when you tap on links. Replace the entire file with the following:

```
ch01_13/android/app/src/main/res/layout/activity_main.xml
<?xml version="1.0" encoding="utf-8"?>
<androidx.fragment.app.FragmentContainerView
    xmlns:android="http://schemas.android.com/apk/res/android"
    xmlns:app="http://schemas.android.com/apk/res-auto"
    android:id="@+id/main"
    android:name="dev.hotwire.navigation.navigator.NavigatorHost"
    android:layout_width="match_parent"
    android:layout_height="match_parent"
    app:defaultNavHost="false" />
```

android:id identifies this node. We'll use this in code to locate the SessionNavHost-Fragment.

android:name is the name of the fragment contained in this view. The value of this property comes from Hotwire Native, hence the dev.hotwire.navigation package prefix.

android:layout_width and android:layout_height tell the view how much space it should take up. We set both values to match_parent to fill the screen.

OK, the view layout is set up to render the Hotwire Native fragment. The next step is telling the app to use this layout and configuring Hotwire Native.

Update the Activity

An Android *activity* is an entry point to the application—it provides a window for a developer to lay out their UI elements and pass user interactions back to code. While complex apps can have multiple activities, we'll stick to a single one.

Expand app, kotlin+java, and then com.masilotti.hikingjournal, and double-click Main-Activity to open it.

As you did with SceneDelegate on iOS, delete the contents of MainActivity. You'll build the entire thing from scratch.

Start by declaring an empty MainActivity class:

ch01_14/android/app/src/main/java/com/masilotti/hikingjournal/MainActivity.kt
```
class MainActivity {
}
```

Then, make the activity inherit from HotwireActivity. As you're typing this class, press Enter to let Android Studio autocomplete it for you. That will automatically import the required class at the top of the file.

ch01_15/android/app/src/main/java/com/masilotti/hikingjournal/MainActivity.kt
```
import dev.hotwire.navigation.activities.HotwireActivity

class MainActivity : HotwireActivity() {
}
```

Note the open and closed parentheses after HotwireActivity. This is called a *constructor invocation*, as it creates an instance of the superclass HotwireActivity. We could pass in different parameters here if needed.

Add an onCreate() function with the override keyword. This overrides a function from the same name as the parent class. onCreate() allows you to initialize the activity and set the view layout—just what we need to render content from Hotwire Native.

As before, let Android Studio autocomplete the function call to automatically import android.os.Bundle.

ch01_16/android/app/src/main/java/com/masilotti/hikingjournal/MainActivity.kt

```
➤ import android.os.Bundle
  import dev.hotwire.navigation.activities.HotwireActivity

  class MainActivity : HotwireActivity() {
➤     override fun onCreate(savedInstanceState: Bundle?) {
➤         super.onCreate(savedInstanceState)
➤     }
  }
```

Now that you have a bit of Swift experience under your belt, the onCreate() function shouldn't look too intimidating. Yes, Kotlin uses fun instead of func to declare the function. But I bet you can guess what the question mark after Bundle means! That's right, it's Kotlin's version of an optional in Swift, a *nullable type*.

Before setting the view, first declare the package at the top of the file. This tells Android Studio where to find non-code resources, like the XML layout file activity_main.xml you updated in the previous section.

ch01_17/android/app/src/main/java/com/masilotti/hikingjournal/MainActivity.kt

```
➤ package com.masilotti.hikingjournal

  import android.os.Bundle
  import dev.hotwire.navigation.activities.HotwireActivity

  class MainActivity : HotwireActivity() {
      override fun onCreate(savedInstanceState: Bundle?) {
          super.onCreate(savedInstanceState)
      }
  }
```

Back in onCreate(savedInstanceState: Bundle?) after the call to super, set the content view with R.layout.activity_main. This finds the resource ("R") in the layout directory named activity_main.xml. Android Studio automatically generates R for you on a successful build.

ch01_18/android/app/src/main/java/com/masilotti/hikingjournal/MainActivity.kt

```
package com.masilotti.hikingjournal

import android.os.Bundle
import dev.hotwire.navigation.activities.HotwireActivity
```

```
class MainActivity : HotwireActivity() {
    override fun onCreate(savedInstanceState: Bundle?) {
        super.onCreate(savedInstanceState)
        setContentView(R.layout.activity_main)
    }
}
```

Before we move on, we need to address a recent change in Android.[10] Starting with Android SDK 35, apps are displayed edge-to-edge—the window fills the entire height of the display and renders behind the status bar at the top of the screen.

To make sure this doesn't overlap our web content, we need to configure our layout to shrink behind the bars.

ch01_19/android/app/src/main/java/com/masilotti/hikingjournal/MainActivity.kt
```
package com.masilotti.hikingjournal

import android.os.Bundle
import android.view.View
import androidx.activity.enableEdgeToEdge
import dev.hotwire.navigation.activities.HotwireActivity
import dev.hotwire.navigation.util.applyDefaultImeWindowInsets

class MainActivity : HotwireActivity() {
    override fun onCreate(savedInstanceState: Bundle?) {
        super.onCreate(savedInstanceState)
        enableEdgeToEdge()
        setContentView(R.layout.activity_main)
        findViewById<View>(R.id.main).applyDefaultImeWindowInsets()
    }
}
```

The view is now configured. Upon launching, the app will attempt to render the Hotwire Native fragment SessionNavHostFragment, declared earlier in activity_main.xml. The last step in this file is to configure Hotwire Native.

Configure a Hotwire Native Navigator

HotwireActivity requires an additional member to be implemented, hence the red squiggle under class MainActivity, indicating an error.

Move your cursor over the squiggle and press ⌥ ↵ to open the context menu. Click "Implement members" and then OK from the next dialog. Android Studio will add a placeholder implementation of the required function, as shown in the screenshot on page 24.

---

10. https://developer.android.com/develop/ui/views/layout/edge-to-edge

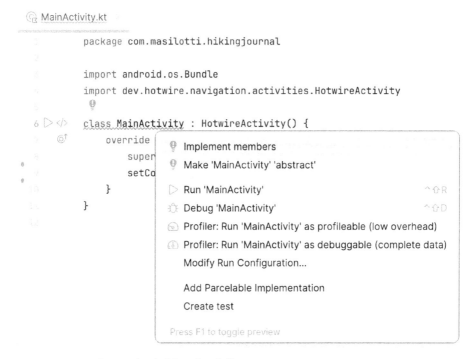

MainActivity.kt will now look like the following:

ch01_20/android/app/src/main/java/com/masilotti/hikingjournal/MainActivity.kt

```
package com.masilotti.hikingjournal

import android.os.Bundle
import android.view.View
import androidx.activity.enableEdgeToEdge
import dev.hotwire.navigation.activities.HotwireActivity
import dev.hotwire.navigation.navigator.NavigatorConfiguration
import dev.hotwire.navigation.util.applyDefaultImeWindowInsets

class MainActivity : HotwireActivity() {
    override fun onCreate(savedInstanceState: Bundle?) {
        super.onCreate(savedInstanceState)
        enableEdgeToEdge()
        setContentView(R.layout.activity_main)
        findViewById<View>(R.id.main).applyDefaultImeWindowInsets()
    }

    override fun navigatorConfigurations(): List<NavigatorConfiguration> {
        TODO("Not yet implemented")
    }
}
```

The red squiggle and any errors are now gone, but we need to address the added TODO note. navigatorConfigurations() requires an array of NavigatorConfiguration instances, one for each web view you want to display. We won't need more than one of these until we get to multiple tabs in Chapter 4, Add a Native Tab Bar, on page 61.

Each NavigatorConfiguration instance requires three parameters:

- name: A unique name to identify the underlying web view.
- startLocation: The URL, as a string, to visit upon launch.
- navigatorHostId: A reference to a FragmentContainerView from the layout XML.

Before implementing the configurations function, we'll mimic the global URL variable from the iOS app. Declare a variable named baseURL outside of MainActivity to ensure access across the codebase.

ch01_21/android/app/src/main/java/com/masilotti/hikingjournal/MainActivity.kt
```kotlin
package com.masilotti.hikingjournal

import android.os.Bundle
import android.view.View
import androidx.activity.enableEdgeToEdge
import dev.hotwire.navigation.activities.HotwireActivity
import dev.hotwire.navigation.navigator.NavigatorConfiguration
import dev.hotwire.navigation.util.applyDefaultImeWindowInsets

const val baseURL = "http://10.0.2.2:3000"

class MainActivity : HotwireActivity() {
    // ...
}
```

The Android emulator runs behind a virtual firewall that isolates it from your development machine. Because of this, you need to use the special alias 10.0.2.2 (instead of localhost, as done with iOS) to loop back to your local Rails server. We'll cover running the app on a physical device in Chapter 9, Deploy to Physical Devices with TestFlight and Play Testing, on page 171.

Now add a single NavigatorConfiguration instance wrapped in listOf() to convert it to an array, like so:

ch01_22/android/app/src/main/java/com/masilotti/hikingjournal/MainActivity.kt
```kotlin
class MainActivity : HotwireActivity() {
    // ...

    override fun navigatorConfigurations() = listOf(
        NavigatorConfiguration(
            name = "main",
            startLocation = "$baseURL/hikes",
            navigatorHostId = R.id.main
        )
    )
}
```

Naming the configuration "main" is arbitrary when we only have a single instance. But we'll want to make sure any additional configurations used for tabs are unique.

For the startLocation parameter, we append the /hikes route to baseURL. This will load the homepage when the app launches.

"$baseURL/hikes" uses a shorthand version of Kotlin's string interpolation for the value of baseURL to build a new URL. In Ruby, this would read #{baseURL}/hikes.

navigatorHostId needs to reference a node from activity_main.xml—Hotwire Native uses this to populate the screen with rendered web content. We named the FragmentContainerView node R.id.main_nav_host in activity_main.xml. ⌘- click on activity_main to navigate to the layout file as a reminder of how this was wired up.

Functions in Kotlin

Functions in Kotlin look pretty similar to functions in Swift.

The following function takes two parameters of type Int and returns another Int:

```kotlin
fun add(x: Int, y: Int): Int {
    return x + y
}
```

We can call functions in Kotlin via their named parameters or via the order they appear, omitting the names.

```kotlin
add(x = 1, y = 2) // Returns 3

add(1, 2) // Returns 3
```

And if the entire function body is a single line of code, we can inline it, just like in Ruby. We're using this shorthand in the navigatorConfigurations() function above.

```kotlin
fun add(x: Int, y: Int) = x + y
```

MainActivity is complete! It should now look like the following:

ch01_24/android/app/src/main/java/com/masilotti/hikingjournal/MainActivity.kt
```kotlin
package com.masilotti.hikingjournal

import android.os.Bundle
import android.view.View
import androidx.activity.enableEdgeToEdge
import dev.hotwire.navigation.activities.HotwireActivity
import dev.hotwire.navigation.navigator.NavigatorConfiguration
import dev.hotwire.navigation.util.applyDefaultImeWindowInsets

const val baseURL = "http://10.0.2.2:3000"

class MainActivity : HotwireActivity() {
```

```
    override fun onCreate(savedInstanceState: Bundle?) {
        super.onCreate(savedInstanceState)
        enableEdgeToEdge()
        setContentView(R.layout.activity_main)
        findViewById<View>(R.id.main).applyDefaultImeWindowInsets()
    }

    override fun navigatorConfigurations() = listOf(
        NavigatorConfiguration(
            name = "main",
            startLocation = "$baseURL/hikes",
            navigatorHostId = R.id.main
        )
    )
}
```

One last bit of configuration, and then we can finally run the Android app. I know, I'm excited (and a bit impatient), too!

Add Internet Permission

Open AndroidManifest.xml by expanding app and then manifests and double-clicking the file. This manifest outlines the permissions, activities, and configuration of the Android app. We need to add the Internet permission and permit access to non-HTTPS resources.

Add the android.permission.INTERNET permission right above the <application>. Then add an android:usesCleartextTraffic property to the <application> node and set it to "true".

ch01_23/android/app/src/main/AndroidManifest.xml
```
<?xml version="1.0" encoding="utf-8"?>
<manifest xmlns:android="http://schemas.android.com/apk/res/android"
    xmlns:tools="http://schemas.android.com/tools">

➤    <uses-permission android:name="android.permission.INTERNET" />

    <application
        android:allowBackup="true"
        android:dataExtractionRules="@xml/data_extraction_rules"
        android:fullBackupContent="@xml/backup_rules"
        android:icon="@mipmap/ic_launcher"
        android:label="@string/app_name"
        android:roundIcon="@mipmap/ic_launcher_round"
        android:supportsRtl="true"
        android:theme="@style/Theme.HikingJournal"
➤        android:usesCleartextTraffic="true"
        tools:targetApi="31">
        <activity
            android:name=".MainActivity"
            android:exported="true">
            <intent-filter>
```

```
        <action android:name="android.intent.action.MAIN" />

        <category android:name="android.intent.category.LAUNCHER" />
      </intent-filter>
    </activity>
  </application>
</manifest>
```

OK, the time has come...run the app again by pressing the green arrow at the top of the screen or by clicking Run → Run 'app'.

You did it! You created a brand-new Android Studio project and integrated Hotwire Native from scratch. Nice work. As you can see, there's a fair amount of configuration required for the Android side of things.

What's Next?

You're only one chapter in, and you've already learned a lot. You now know how to create new Xcode and Android Studio projects, how to integrate the Hotwire Native framework, and enough native code to build bare-bones hybrid apps. But we haven't yet talked about perhaps the biggest benefit of Hotwire Native.

In the next chapter, we'll explore different ways of driving your mobile apps *without native code changes*. You'll learn how to update content rendered by the apps and how to access some native functionality like the camera and photo library.

## CHAPTER 2

Control Your Apps with Rails

The biggest benefit of using Hotwire Native to build mobile apps is that you are rendering content directly from the Rails server. Make a change to your Rails code, and boom—the iOS and Android apps get that update automatically. But it can be hard to appreciate that magic until you see it for yourself.

This chapter covers different techniques and approaches to drive content and behavior in the apps directly from the server. Everything in this chapter will be Ruby on Rails code.

Specifically, you'll learn how to do the following:

1. Dynamically set a native title via HTML.
2. Hide the navigation bar with conditional Ruby.
3. Hide the navigation bar with CSS.
4. Add back in missing elements.
5. Keep users signed in between app launches.
6. Access the user's Camera and Photos on iOS.
7. Access the user's Camera and Photos on Android.

But before we explore each technique, I want to show you something—probably the most exciting part about building Hotwire Native apps.

First, visit https://localhost:3000 in your browser and open Xcode to run the iOS app. Both show the hike index page as expected.

Now add a new HTML element to the code that powers this page, app/views/hikes/index.html.erb, like so:

```
ch02_01/rails/app/views/hikes/index.html.erb
<%= render "shared/header", title: "Hikes" %>

<div class="container">
```

```
➤    <div class="alert alert-primary" role="alert">
➤      New content added from the Rails codebase.
➤    </div>
➤  </div>

   <%# ... %>
```

Refresh the page in the browser to see the updated content. Boring, right? That's what's expected of websites! But now for the magic...

Back in the iOS simulator, click and drag the mouse from near the top of the screen down toward the bottom. You'll see a little spinner start filling in at the top. Once it fills, let go, and the page will refresh. And there's the content you added to the server!

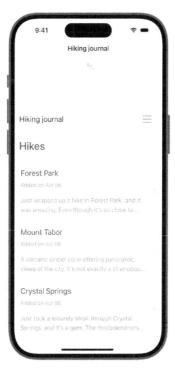
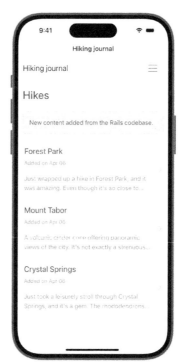

The magic is that this didn't require any native code changes, a rebuild of the app, *or* a deploy to the App Store. Whatever content your Rails server renders, your apps will always show on the screen.

I'm using an alert to keep things simple. But the real magic comes from the mindset shift—you could add an entire new feature to the Rails codebase and the iOS and Android apps will get them...entirely for free.

Ready to learn the first technique? Let's go!

Dynamically Set a Native Title via HTML

We'll cover the first technique in our list—dynamically setting the native title via HTML—by way of addressing the repetitive Hiking Journal text at the top center of the screen. This *title* is most similar to an <h1> tag on the web, a string that represents the content on the screen. Right now, every screen shows the same text at the top. It would look a lot nicer, and would actually be more useful, if that title displayed something a bit more dynamic.

The title lives inside the native navigation bar, highlighted in the left image that follows. The web content rendered from the server is highlighted on the right.

Under the hood, Hotwire Native sets this title element to the HTML's <title> tag when the page loads. And it does so automatically! This means we can update the string directly from our HTML code—no additional Swift or Kotlin required.

But how do we set a different <title> for each page? I like to use a Rails helper: content_for.

content_for

content_for[1] allows you to insert content into named blocks in your layout. Think of it as a placeholder for content created later in the page rendering cycle.

---

1. https://guides.rubyonrails.org/layouts_and_rendering.html#using-the-content-for-method

You'll interact with content_for in two ways: to set content and to retrieve content. You set content by providing two parameters: the identifier of the content and the content itself. Then, you retrieve it by only passing in the identifier, as follows:

```erb
<%# Set content. %>
<% content_for :name, "Joe" %>

<%# Retrieve (and render) the content. %>
<%= content_for :name %>
```

You can also pass a block to set more complex content, like HTML:

```erb
<%# Set content from a block. %>
<% content_for :complex_html do %>
  <%= link_to "Home", root_path %>
<% end %>

<%# Render the block content. %>
<%= content_for :complex_html %>
```

If no content has been set for an identifier, then content_for returns nil. This can be used to provide a default value to fall back to by chaining it with ||.

```erb
<%= content_for(:name) || "Someone" %>
```

Setting Dynamic Titles

Using content_for, let's set the HTML title of the hike page to the name of the hike. This will, in turn, set the native title of the view controller in Hotwire Native.

First, refactor the application.html.erb by replacing the contents of the <title> tag with content_for. Don't forget a default value!

```erb
ch02_02/rails/app/views/layouts/application.html.erb
<!DOCTYPE html>
<html>
  <head>
    <title><%= content_for(:title) || "Hiking Journal" %></title>
    <meta name="viewport" content="width=device-width,initial-scale=1">
    <%= csrf_meta_tags %>
    <%= csp_meta_tag %>

    <%# ... %>
  </head>

  <body>
    <%# ... %>
  </body>
</html>
```

The hike show template renders a small partial at the top of the file: shared/_header.html.erb.

ch02_03/rails/app/views/hikes/show.html.erb
```
<%= render "shared/header", title: @hike.name %>

<div class="container">
  <%# ... %>

</div>
```

Open that partial, app/views/shared/_header.html.erb, and use content_for to set the title of the page to the name of the hike via the title local variable.

ch02_04/rails/app/views/shared/_header.html.erb
```
<% content_for :title, title %>

<div class="container">
  <h1 class="my-4 pt-md-4"><%= title %></h1>
</div>
```

Run the app and navigate to a hike page. The title of the hike now appears as the native title of the view controller. And because you used content_for to set it dynamically, every single hike page gets this functionality.

Here's what that looks like on iOS (on the left) and Android (on the right).

Hide the Navigation Bar with Conditional Ruby

Up next is addressing the web-based navigation bar that appears on every page. On mobile web, this navigation bar is a convenient way to display the title of the website and a few important links, like a hamburger menu of sorts. But your native apps have their own navigation bar. Native ones! There's no need to display the same content twice in the apps. In this section, you'll hide specific web elements for the Hotwire Native apps.

First, we need a way to identify the Hotwire Native app from other web requests. Lucky for us, the turbo-rails gem[2] comes with a helper to do exactly that. The Rails app is already using the gem, so no changes are needed on your end.

For the curious, here's what the code looks like under the hood of the gem:

```
# turbo-rails/app/controllers/turbo/native/navigation.rb
module Turbo::Native::Navigation
  extend ActiveSupport::Concern

  included do
    helper_method :hotwire_native_app?, :turbo_native_app?
  end

  def hotwire_native_app?
    request.user_agent.to_s.match?(/(Turbo|Hotwire) Native/)
  end

  # ...
end
```

This exposes the helper method hotwire_native_app? to our Rails controllers and views in order to easily identify requests from Hotwire Native apps. If the user agent includes the "Hotwire Native" string, then the method returns true. Hotwire Native automatically adds "Hotwire Native" (and "Turbo Native," for backward compatibility with the old library) to the user agent on every request, so no additional code is needed in the apps.

Use this method in app/views/shared/_navbar.html.erb to skip the rendering of the navigation bar for Hotwire Native apps, as follows:

ch02_05/rails/app/views/shared/_navbar.html.erb
```
➤ <% unless hotwire_native_app? %>
    <nav class="navbar bg-body-tertiary">
      <div class="container">
        <%# ... %>
      </div>
    </nav>
➤ <% end %>
```

The navigation bar is now hidden from the native apps but is still visible on mobile web, as shown in the screenshot on page 35.

---

2.   https://github.com/hotwired/turbo-rails

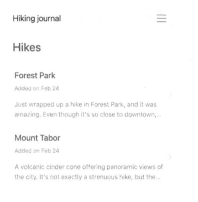
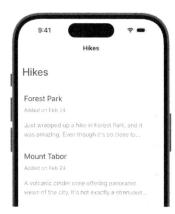

Using `hotwire_native_app?` to conditionally render content works great. You're given full control over what to send to the native apps and what to only render on mobile web. But this approach has a trade-off. Sending different HTML, depending on the user agent, can break caching. To know which HTML to send, the cache now *also* needs to be aware of the user agent of the request.

Personally, I'd rather not double the size of my cache only to hide elements in the apps. Let's take a look at a different approach to hiding the navigation bar, which sends the same HTML no matter the user agent—no changes to your caching are required.

Hide the Navigation Bar with CSS

Bootstrap uses responsive breakpoints[3] to conditionally apply styles to different screen sizes. For example, applying the `d-none` class to an element hides it on all devices by setting the `display` property to `none`. And throwing `md`, the keyword for medium, in between creates `d-md-none`. Applying this class hides the element only on screen sizes of size medium or larger.

You can follow this guidance to create a similar class for Hotwire Native apps: `d-hotwire-native-none`.

First, remove the `hotwire_native_app?` conditional and add the new nav class `d-hotwire-native-none`:

ch02_06/rails/app/views/shared/_navbar.html.erb
```
<nav class="navbar d-hotwire-native-none bg-body-tertiary">
  <div class="container">
    <%# ... %>
  </div>
</nav>
```

---

3. https://getbootstrap.com/docs/5.3/layout/breakpoints/

Next, create a new CSS file in app/assets/stylesheets and name it native.css. Add the new CSS class d-hotwire-native-none here to hide content:

```
ch02_07/rails/app/assets/stylesheets/native.css
.d-hotwire-native-none {
  display: none !important;
}
```

You only want to include these CSS overrides for Hotwire Native apps. Using the hotwire_native_app? helper from earlier, you can link to the stylesheet to do exactly that! Update the application layout as follows to conditionally link to the native stylesheet:

```
ch02_08/rails/app/views/layouts/application.html.erb
<!DOCTYPE html>
<html>
  <head>
    <%# ... %>

    <%= stylesheet_link_tag "application", "data-turbo-track": "reload" %>
    <% if hotwire_native_app? %>
      <%= stylesheet_link_tag "native", "data-turbo-track": "reload" %>
    <% end %>

    <%# ... %>
  </head>

  <body>
    <%# ... %>
  </body>
</html>
```

You now have a place to put all of your conditional CSS that *augments* your native apps—the new stylesheet. It can override existing styles or add new ones like you just did. And the best part? You no longer need to submit a new version of your app to make style changes. You can simply update native.css as if it were any other stylesheet, and your app gets the updates immediately.

Before we move on to discuss how to accomplish this with other CSS frameworks, let's first address the double title problem in the apps.

Hide the <h1>

Your apps currently show two Forest Park titles and two Hikes titles. Each screen now renders this page title in the native navigation bar *and* in the <h1> tag right after it, as shown in the screenshot on page 37.

To fix this, add the same CSS class d-hotwire-native-none in shared/_header.html.erb to hide the <h1> tags:

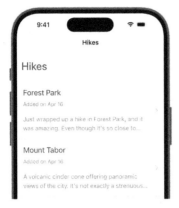

ch02_09/rails/app/views/shared/_header.html.erb

```
<% content_for :title, title %>

<div class="container">
  <h1 class="d-hotwire-native-none my-4 pt-md-4"><%= title %></h1>
</div>
```

Ah, much better.

Custom Variants for Tailwind CSS

The native.css approach works great if you only need to add a few styles manually. But if you want something a bit more dynamic, and if you are using Tailwind CSS in your Rails app, there's another approach to consider.

> **Tailwind CSS**
>
> For those who are unfamiliar with Tailwind CSS, here's a bit of background: Tailwind CSS[a] is a utility-first CSS framework. This means you won't find semantic classes like card or even container here. Instead, it uses a plethora of tiny ones like flex, pt-4, text-center, and rotate-90.

> The benefit of using Tailwind is that you can use these utility classes to compose *any* design, directly in your markup, without having to also juggle and maintain CSS by hand.
>
> Where Bootstrap has responsive breakpoints, Tailwind CSS has *variants*. These handle not only screen sizes but also hover state, color scheme, and more. Variants are declared with the variant name, followed by a colon, and then the class name to apply.
>
> Here are some examples:
>
> ```
> <div class="bg-white md:bg-black">
>   White background on small screens, black on medium and larger.
> </div>
>
> <div class="text-black dark:text-white">
>   Black text by default, white text when dark mode is enabled.
> </div>
> ```
>
> ---
>
> a. https://tailwindcss.com

With Tailwind CSS, you can create a custom modifier that only applies to Hotwire Native apps. Normally, we identify these requests by inspecting the user agent. But Tailwind CSS modifiers are written in CSS, which can't access the request or the user agent.

The Rails app in this book uses Bootstrap. But if your app is using Tailwind CSS, you can identify the requests by adding the data-hotwire-native-app attribute to the <html> tag in your application layout:

ch02_10/rails/app/views/layouts/application.html.erb
```
<!DOCTYPE html>
<html <%= "data-hotwire-native" if hotwire_native_app? %>>
  <head>
    <%# ... %>
  </head>

  <body>
    <%# ... %>
  </body>
</html>
```

For Tailwind CSS v4, use @variant in tailwind/application.css to create the new modifiers.

ch02_10/rails/app/assets/stylesheets/tailwind/application.css
```
@import "tailwindcss";

@custom-variant hotwire-native {
    html[data-hotwire-native] & {
```

```
➤            @slot
➤        }
➤    }
➤
➤    @custom-variant not-hotwire-native {
➤        html:not([data-hotwire-native]) & {
➤            @slot
➤        }
➤    }
```

And for Tailwind CSS v3, use addVariant in tailwind.config.js.

ch02_10/rails/tailwind.config.js
```
/** @type {import('tailwindcss').Config} */
module.exports = {
  content: [],
  theme: {
    extend: {},
  },
  plugins: [
➤    ({ addVariant }) => {
➤      addVariant("hotwire-native",
➤        "html[data-hotwire-native-app] &"),
➤      addVariant("not-hotwire-native",
➤        "html:not([data-hotwire-native-app]) &")
➤    },
  ],
}
```

You can now prefix any Tailwind CSS class with hotwire-native: to only apply that style to Hotwire Native apps. And you can use not-hotwire-native: to apply a style to everything *but* Hotwire Native apps:

```
<div class="bg-white hotwire-native:bg-black">
  White background on web, black on Hotwire Native apps.
</div>

<div class="text-black not-hotwire-native:text-white">
  Black text on Hotwire Native apps, white text on web.
</div>
```

Remember that this note was only an example; the Rails app we're working with doesn't have Tailwind CSS installed.

Add Missing Elements

You've now hidden the web-based navigation bar from Hotwire Native apps, as shown in the screenshot on page 40. But there were valuable links in there that are no longer accessible!

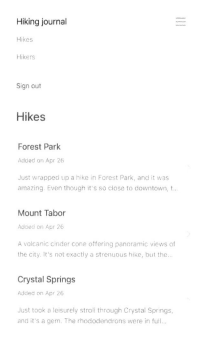

It's no longer possible for users of your app to sign in and out. And you've effectively removed the links to the Hikes and Hikers pages. Let's add back those sign-in and sign-out links. We'll address the Hikes and Hikers navigation links when we explore native tabs in Chapter 4, Add a Native Tab Bar, on page 61.

First, add a new style (d-hotwire-native-block) to native.css that *shows* elements only on Hotwire Native apps:

ch02_11/rails/app/assets/stylesheets/native.css
```
.d-hotwire-native-none {
  display: none !important;
}

.d-hotwire-native-block {
  display: block !important;
}
```

Then add two new buttons to the hike index page: one for signing in and one for signing out. Use the new d-hotwire-native-block class to have them hidden on the web but visible in the apps:

ch02_12/rails/app/views/hikes/index.html.erb
```
<%= render "shared/header", title: "Hikes" %>
<%# ... %>

<div class="container d-flex justify-content-between gap-2 mt-4">
```

```erb
<% if user_signed_in? %>
  <%= link_to "Add a hike", new_hike_path,
    class: "btn btn-primary flex-grow-1 flex-sm-grow-0" %>
  <%= link_to "Sign out", session_path,
    class: "btn btn-outline-danger d-none d-hotwire-native-block",
    data: {
      turbo_method: "delete",
      turbo_confirm: "Sign out?"
    } %>
<% else %>
  <div class="flex-grow-1">
    <%= link_to "Sign in", new_session_path,
      class: "btn btn-outline-primary d-none d-hotwire-native-block" %>
  </div>
<% end %>
</div>
```

Combining d-none with d-hotwire-native-block adds the display: none; style on the web but overwrites it with display: block !important; in the apps. Perfect!

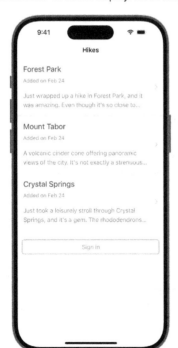 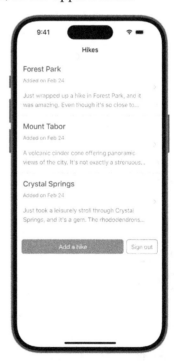

You've now learned two techniques to drive mobile app content from the server code: you're dynamically setting the native title and conditionally rendering HTML content. Before we move on to driving *behavior*, let's fix an innocent but impactful bug.

Keep Users Signed In Between App Launches

Have you noticed that every time you launch the app you have to sign in again? Mobile app users expect to remain signed in even after they close or background an app. Let's fix that.

Check out the Authentication concern[4] in the Rails codebase. This module is included in ApplicationController to authenticate users. The #sign_in method persists the user's ID to an encrypted cookie when they sign in.

ch02_13/rails/app/controllers/concerns/authentication.rb
```ruby
module Authentication
  extend ActiveSupport::Concern

  included do
    helper_method :current_user, :user_signed_in?
  end

  def sign_in(user)
    Current.user = user
    cookies.encrypted[:user_id] = user.id
  end

  # ...
end
```

By default, a cookie set this way in Rails "will be deleted when the user's browser is closed."[5] Every time the app is launched, it is considered "closing" the browser, so we get signed out.

Instead of these ephemeral cookies, we want long-lived ones. We can make the cookie last 20 years (essentially "forever") by using the permanent method, like so:

ch02_14/rails/app/controllers/concerns/authentication.rb
```ruby
module Authentication
  extend ActiveSupport::Concern

  included do
    helper_method :current_user, :user_signed_in?
  end

  def sign_in(user)
    Current.user = user
    cookies.permanent.encrypted[:user_id] = user.id
  end

  # ...
end
```

---

4. https://api.rubyonrails.org/v7.1.3.2/classes/ActiveSupport/Concern.html
5. https://api.rubyonrails.org/v8.0.0/classes/ActionDispatch/Cookies.html

Run the app, sign in, and then re-run the app. You'll now remain signed in until you explicitly tap the Sign out button at the bottom of the screen.

I love this example because it illustrates an important piece of the Hotwire Native puzzle. You just fixed a pretty severe bug without writing a single line of native code. *And* without deploying a new build for the App Store.

Up next is driving *behavior* from the server, specifically, accessing the user's photo library.

Access the Camera and Photos on iOS

Mobile apps often want access to information stored on the user's device, such as when using the camera or photo library for image uploads. This is another area where Hotwire Native shines. We can trigger fully baked, native flows without writing *any* native code. All we need is the right HTML markup—iOS will take care of the rest!

Run the iOS app from Xcode and sign in. Then tap "Add a hike" and, to set the image, tap the Choose File button in the form.

Select a photo from the library, give it a name and description, and click Save, as shown in the screenshot on page 44.

And you have a fully featured image uploader *completely for free*! No Swift code was required to make this work. All Hotwire Native needed was an HTML <input> tag with type="file" that accepts images. Rails adds this for us automatically when using the file_field helper on an attachment, as shown here:

ch02_15/rails/app/views/hikes/_form.html.erb
```
<%= form_with model: hike, class: "row g-3 mt-1" do |form| %>
  <%# ... %>

  <div>
    <%= form.label :image, class: "form-label" %>

    <% if hike.image.attached? %>
      <%= image_tag hike.image, class: "img-thumbnail" %>
      <%= form.hidden_field :image, value: hike.image.signed_id %>
    <% end %>

    <%= form.file_field :image,
      accept: "image/jpg,image/jpeg,image/png",
      class: "form-control mt-2" %>
  </div>

  <%# ... %>
  <div class="d-grid d-sm-flex justify-content-sm-end mt-4">
    <%= form.submit "Save", class: "btn btn-primary" %>
  </div>
<% end %>
```

Next, we'll move on to the Android side of things.

Access the Camera and Photos on Android

Just like on iOS, you don't need to do anything to access the user's camera or photo library on Android! Everything will work out of the box with the <input type="file"/> tag from the server.

Tapping the Choose File button when editing a hike presents a user with the option to choose between the camera or the photo library.

And tapping the Camera option in the emulator gives you a cute little dancing robot. Look at them go!

What's Next?

Your apps are really coming together. In this chapter, you've learned different ways to drive content and behavior directly from the server. You dynamically set the native title via HTML, hid the navigation bar with CSS, accessed the user's photo library, and more.

These apps technically work—you can navigate between screens, sign in and out, and even add new hikes. But there are a few rough edges, especially around workflows dealing with submitting forms. In the next chapter, you'll learn how to improve the form UX via the path configuration to make the apps feel a bit more native.

## CHAPTER 3

Navigate Gracefully with Path Configuration

You've built the foundation for your native apps, and you understand how Hotwire Native drives the content directly from the Rails server. Now, let's improve the user experience. The current Hotwire Native integration does enough to function, but it leaves a lot to be desired.

Take, for example, the process of creating a new hike. Launch the app, sign in, and tap "Add a hike" at the bottom. Fill out the form and tap Save to add the hike to the database. A new screen will push onto the stack showing the hike data you entered—flash message included!

But try navigating back by tapping "Add a hike" in the upper left. Notice how you see the same filled-out form from before? For a mobile app, that behavior's quite odd. In this chapter, you'll address that with Hotwire Native's *path configuration*.

Specifically, you'll learn these things:

1. How modals are used in native apps.
2. What path configuration is.
3. How to integrate the apps with remote path configuration.

Let's get started with modals!

Routing Modals

To remedy the issue with the form, you can use a *modal* to break context and encourage a distinct, narrowly scoped task. With mobile apps, modals are screens that are presented from the bottom—they don't slide in from the side, which is a traditional mobile navigation action. This distinction helps the user differentiate between two workflows.

Here are a couple of example modals, iOS on the left and Android on the right, from the Hotwire Native demo apps.

Hotwire Native supports a few navigation options out of the box, modals being one of them. This chapter will cover how to effectively use modals and other navigation techniques to create a better user experience in your apps—one that more closely resembles how users expect native apps to behave.

Remember, a big benefit of Hotwire Native is that it keeps your business logic in one place: the Rails server. We don't want to hardcode into the apps which screens get presented as modals—that detail should come from the server. Instead, you wire up rules that map different URL paths to different navigation patterns. And you do this via *path configuration*.

Path configuration is represented as a JSON file hosted on the server. Based on the settings you configure for this JSON file, your native apps can change their behavior. You'll use path configuration to tell your apps how to present different screens. And because the JSON file lives on the server, not in the app, you're free to update this file in between releases to the app stores to skip the review process.

For each platform, you'll first set up the path configuration. Then, you'll wire up the clients. Ready? Let's dive in.

Set Up iOS Path Configuration

To set up iOS path configuration, first create a new route (or endpoint) on the server that points to /configurations/ios_v1.

ch03_01/rails/config/routes.rb
```ruby
Rails.application.routes.draw do
  resource :session, only: %i[new create destroy]

  resources :hikes do
    resource :map, only: :show
    resources :likes, only: %w[create destroy]
  end

  resources :users, only: :index do
    resources :hikes, only: :index, controller: :user_hikes
  end

  resources :configurations, only: [] do
    get :ios_v1, on: :collection
  end

  root "hikes#index"
end
```

You'll want different path configurations for each platform, so prefix this one with ios. I also like to version the resource just in case a future version of the app introduces a breaking change, hence the v1.

Next, create a new Rails controller that maps to this route. For now, respond with an empty JSON object.

ch03_02/rails/app/controllers/configurations_controller.rb
```
class ConfigurationsController < ApplicationController
  def ios_v1
    render json: {
    }
  end
end
```

Path configuration is comprised of two parts: settings and rules keys. The settings key isn't used directly by the framework. It's provided for developers to define and manage their own app-specific configuration. Anything you want to configure on the server but apply in the app belongs here.

This chapter focuses on the rules key—this is where we map URL paths to navigation options. Think of these rules as a way to abstract behavior from hardcoded URLs.

A completely empty path configuration for iOS looks like the following:

ch03_03/rails/app/controllers/configurations_controller.rb
```
class ConfigurationsController < ApplicationController
  def ios_v1
    render json: {
      settings: {},
      rules: [
      ]
    }
  end
end
```

This configures no custom settings and no rules. Even though we won't use any custom iOS settings in this book, we still need to include the empty object ("hash," in Ruby terms) for Hotwire Native to work correctly.

The rules key holds an array of objects, each with two keys: patterns and properties. The patterns key matches URL paths via a regular expression, and the properties key applies different behaviors to the route.

Hotwire Native automatically handles a few different properties out of the box. For now, we'll focus on the *context* property, which tells the framework if the new screen should be presented as a modal or not.

Add a rule to present all forms as modals, like so:

ch03_04/rails/app/controllers/configurations_controller.rb
```
class ConfigurationsController < ApplicationController
  def ios_v1
```

```
      render json: {
        settings: {},
        rules: [
➤         {
➤           patterns: [
➤             "/new$",
➤             "/edit$"
➤           ],
➤           properties: {
➤             context: "modal"
➤           }
➤         }
        ]
      }
    end
end
```

By convention, forms in Rails end in /new or /edit, which can be mapped as a pattern to a regex with a trailing dollar sign, which indicates the end of a string.

Now, every time a page is visited where the URL path ends in /new or /edit, the context property will be set to "modal". And under the hood, Hotwire Native is aware of this special property and will present the screen as a modal.

The benefit of using remote path configuration is that you can change the patterns key without releasing a new version of the app. For example, let's say you want to display a brand-new user profile screen as a modal. Simply add /profile to the array, and you're done! No need to even touch the native code, let alone submit a new release to the app stores.

Before your iOS app can apply these rules, you need to wire up a remote path configuration.

Wire Up the iOS Client

Back in the iOS app, you need to tell Hotwire Native where this configuration lives.

Path configuration should be set up before we create our Navigator in SceneDelegate. A great place for this, and any future configuration, is in AppDelegate. Open that file and delete code until you are left with the following.

ch03_05/ios/HikingJournal/AppDelegate.swift
```swift
import UIKit

@main
class AppDelegate: UIResponder, UIApplicationDelegate {
    func application(
        _ application: UIApplication,
```

```
        didFinishLaunchingWithOptions launchOptions:
        [UIApplication.LaunchOptionsKey: Any]?
    ) -> Bool {
        return true
    }
}
```

This function, application(_:didFinishLaunchingWithOptions:), is the first thing that's called when our app launches, even before SceneDelegate is created.

SceneDelegate vs. AppDelegate

Multiple instances of the same iOS app can be run on devices with larger screens, like iPads. AppDelegate manages the global application and state whereas SceneDelegate manages each instance, or scene.

Our app will always assume a single scene. So we'll always have a single instance of SceneDelegate (and AppDelegate).

Import Hotwire Native and set up the path configuration with an empty array in AppDelegate.

ch03_06/ios/HikingJournal/AppDelegate.swift
```
import HotwireNative
import UIKit

@main
class AppDelegate: UIResponder, UIApplicationDelegate {
    func application(
        _ application: UIApplication,
        didFinishLaunchingWithOptions launchOptions:
        [UIApplication.LaunchOptionsKey: Any]?
    ) -> Bool {
        Hotwire.loadPathConfiguration(from: [
        ])

        return true
    }
}
```

Next, tell the PathConfiguration where to find the resource on the server.

ch03_07/ios/HikingJournal/AppDelegate.swift
```
import HotwireNative
import UIKit

@main
class AppDelegate: UIResponder, UIApplicationDelegate {
    func application(
        _ application: UIApplication,
        didFinishLaunchingWithOptions launchOptions:
        [UIApplication.LaunchOptionsKey: Any]?
    ) -> Bool {
```

```
      Hotwire.loadPathConfiguration(from: [
          .server(baseURL.appending(path: "configurations/ios_v1.json"))
      ])

      return true
   }
}
```

/configurations/ios_v1.json is appended to the app's homepage to create the route. See the .server() option? This tells Hotwire Native to fetch this JSON from a remote endpoint, parse the file, and apply the rules when the app is launched.

Run the app and create a new hike. Clicking the New button presents the hike form in a modal.

Seeing the new hike form in this way helps break down the flow of the app and sends the user on a little side quest. Submitting a valid form dismisses the modal and pushes a new screen.

On the Rails side, the hikes controller didn't do anything special. If you look at the code, it looks pretty...well, boring. It just redirected to the show page!

ch03_08/rails/app/controllers/hikes_controller.rb
```ruby
class HikesController < ApplicationController
  def create
    @hike = Hike.new(hike_params)
    if @hike.save
      redirect_to @hike, notice: "Hike added."
    else
      render :new, status: :unprocessable_entity
    end
  end
end
```

Hotwire Native is smart enough to "catch" that redirect and render it in a new screen. And because the new hike route, /hikes/:id, doesn't have any special path configuration, the modal gets dismissed and the show page gets pushed on the main, non-modal stack.

There's another bonus we get with Hotwire Native related to forms. Submitting an invalid form renders the flash message with all of our errors, just like we expect on the web:

Neat!

Now, when you navigate back to the index page, you'll see the new hike already loaded at the top, as shown in the screenshot on page 55.

But how did Hotwire Native know to fetch a new version of this page from the server? With some clever use of the *snapshot cache*.

The Hotwire Native Snapshot Cache

Hotwire Native employs a few tricks to make apps feel more like native ones. One of those is the snapshot cache, which ensures previously fetched pages appear to load instantly. Try it out with the iOS app you're creating. Navigate to a page, then tap the back button. Notice how the content is rendered right away, without a spinner or delay?

This is because a screenshot is taken of every single page. When you navigate from one page to another, the snapshot of the previous page is written to the cache. When a user navigates back, the library loads this image from memory, so it appears like the content loads instantly.

Under the hood, Hotwire Native is moving a single web view between view controllers. Web views take a long time to spin up, so sharing one between screens further increases the perceived speed of the app. The snapshot cache gives users a near-native experience when navigating forward and backward around the app.

But as with all caches, they eventually need to be busted. If not, you might end up displaying stale or out-of-date content to your users.

Clearing the snapshot cache ensures that tapping the back button makes a fresh request to the server, populating the screen with the latest data. Every time the app performs a non-GET request, like when submitting a form, Hotwire Native will bust the cache.

With iOS path configuration wired up, let's shift gears to Android.

Set Up Android Path Configuration

First, create a new route in the Rails app that points to an Android version of path configuration.

ch03_10/rails/config/routes.rb
```
Rails.application.routes.draw do
  # ...

  resources :configurations, only: [] do
    get :ios_v1, on: :collection
➤   get :android_v1, on: :collection
  end
end
```

Open ConfigurationsController.rb and copy-paste the body of ios_v1 into a new method, android_v1.

ch03_11/rails/app/controllers/configurations_controller.rb
```
class ConfigurationsController < ApplicationController
  def ios_v1
    # ...
  end

➤ def android_v1
➤   render json: {
➤     settings: {},
➤     rules: [
➤       {
➤         patterns: [
➤           "/new$",
➤           "/edit$"
➤         ],
➤         properties: {
➤           context: "modal"
➤         }
➤       }
➤     ]
➤   }
➤ end
end
```

This configures the Android app to display all forms as modals—identified by routes ending in /new or /edit. Just like the iOS app.

Unlike iOS, once the path configuration is in place, Android needs an additional rule to function correctly: a rule that matches *all* URL paths. Add the following rule above the one that already exists:

```
ch03_12/rails/app/controllers/configurations_controller.rb
class ConfigurationsController < ApplicationController
  def ios_v1
    # ...
  end

  def android_v1
    render json: {
      settings: {},
      rules: [
        {
          patterns: [
            ".*"
          ],
          properties: {
          }
        },
        {
          patterns: [
            "/new$",
            "/edit$"
          ],
          properties: {
            context: "modal"
          }
        }
      ]
    }
  end
end
```

This is known as the *wildcard rule* because it matches everything. Path configuration rules are applied from top to bottom, applying properties to all rules that match. So any properties assigned here will also be included in URL paths matching rules that appear later.

For this rule, set the uri property and enable pull-to-refresh like so:

```
ch03_13/rails/app/controllers/configurations_controller.rb
class ConfigurationsController < ApplicationController
  def ios_v1
    # ...
  end

  def android_v1
    render json: {
      settings: {},
      rules: [
        {
          patterns: [
            ".*"
```

```
        ],
        properties: {
          uri: "hotwire://fragment/web",
          pull_to_refresh_enabled: true
        }
      },
      {
        # ...
      }
    ]
  }
  end
end
```

The uri property ensures the default Hotwire Native WebFragment class is rendered for every screen. Don't worry about this just yet, as we'll explore this in detail in Chapter 6, Render Native Screens with Jetpack Compose, on page 103.

Enabling pull-to-refresh allows users to drag their finger down the web view to trigger a reload of the page, a common and expected action on Android apps. But this action can often conflict with dismissing screens that are presented as modals. So go ahead and disable this feature for modals.

ch03_14/rails/app/controllers/configurations_controller.rb
```ruby
class ConfigurationsController < ApplicationController
  def ios_v1
    # ...
  end

  def android_v1
    render json: {
      settings: {},
      rules: [
        # ...
        {
          patterns: [
            "/new$",
            "/edit$"
          ],
          properties: {
            context: "modal",
            pull_to_refresh_enabled: false
          }
        }
      ]
    }
  end
end
```

Remote path configuration is in place. All that's left is to tell the Android app where it is so Hotwire Native can fetch, parse, and apply the rules.

Wire Up the Android Client

Open MainActivity.kt. At the end of the onCreate() function, configure Hotwire via loadPathConfiguration(), making sure to import Hotwire Native and PathConfiguration from the library.

```
ch03_15/android/app/src/main/java/com/masilotti/hikingjournal/MainActivity.kt
package com.masilotti.hikingjournal

import android.os.Bundle
import android.view.View
import androidx.activity.enableEdgeToEdge
➤ import dev.hotwire.core.config.Hotwire
➤ import dev.hotwire.core.turbo.config.PathConfiguration
import dev.hotwire.navigation.activities.HotwireActivity
import dev.hotwire.navigation.navigator.NavigatorConfiguration
import dev.hotwire.navigation.util.applyDefaultImeWindowInsets

const val baseURL = "http://10.0.2.2:3000"

class MainActivity : HotwireActivity() {
    override fun onCreate(savedInstanceState: Bundle?) {
        super.onCreate(savedInstanceState)
        enableEdgeToEdge()
        setContentView(R.layout.activity_main)
        findViewById<View>(R.id.main).applyDefaultImeWindowInsets()

➤       Hotwire.loadPathConfiguration(
➤           context = this,
➤           location = PathConfiguration.Location(
➤               remoteFileUrl = "$baseURL/configurations/android_v1.json"
➤           )
➤       )
    }
    // ...
}
```

Run the app, sign in, and click the "Add a hike" button at the bottom of the screen. Note how this fragment slides up from the bottom instead of from the right, just like modals on iOS. We also get an X button in the upper left to dismiss the modal if we wish, as shown in the screenshot on page 60. Nice!

What's Next?

This chapter covered how to set up remote path configuration for iOS and Android in order to route forms as modals. As a navigation option that Hotwire Native supports out of the box, modals create better user experiences and make the apps feel more native. And because we kept the logic and configuration on the server, our app is now more resilient to future changes and easier to maintain. But routing forms as modals is the tip of the iceberg. Remote path configuration can be used to route a whole lot more, like native screens powered by SwiftUI in Chapter 5, Render Native Screens with SwiftUI, on page 81, and Jetpack Compose in Chapter 6, Render Native Screens with Jetpack Compose, on page 103.

We still have a problem to resolve with our apps. Remember when we hid the web-based navigation bar in Chapter 2, Control Your Apps with Rails, on page 29? That had important links to the "Hikes" and "Hikers" pages. And right now, users of the apps can't access them. Now that you've learned how path configuration can route different pages to different behaviors, you're ready to explore adding native tabs to your apps—a common navigation pattern on native iOS and Android apps.

## CHAPTER 4

Add a Native Tab Bar

Tab bars are one of the most common navigation patterns in native apps. Open up a few apps on your phone. Odds are a good portion of them have a tab bar at the bottom of the screen. Because they are so prevalent, users understand how to use them and expect them in their apps.

For example, this row of buttons along the bottom of an iOS app is the tab bar. In the built-in Clock app, each tab is a different use case or feature. World Clock is used to check what time it is in different time zones, and Timers is used to manage, well, timers.

This chapter covers how to add tabs to your Hotwire Native apps. You'll clean up your iOS and Android directories to prepare for tabs and then configure a tab for each link in the navigation bar.

As before, you'll first build the feature on iOS and then move over to Android.

But before we dive in, let's clean up our workspace a bit. You're going to be adding a few new files to the project in this chapter, so let's make sure everything has its own space.

Clean Up the iOS Directories

I like to organize my Xcode projects like Rails applications. By keeping them in line with each other, I have one less context switch to make when swapping back and forth between the codebases. This means controllers in a Controllers folder, views in a Views folder, and so on, with the one exception: iOS uses capitalized camel case instead of lowercased underscores.

First, from the Project Navigator in Xcode, rename the HikingJournal that has the folder icon to App. Click it once, and then press the ↵ key. Type "App" and hit ↵ again.

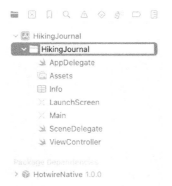

Now, create a new nested folder by right-clicking App and selecting New Folder from the context menu. Name this folder Delegates. Click and drag AppDelegate and SceneDelegate into this folder, as shown in the screenshot on page 63.

Create a second nested folder under App and name it Resources. Click and drag Main, Assets, LaunchScreen, and Info into this folder.

We aren't using ViewController, so go ahead and delete that by right-clicking it and selecting Delete. When Xcode asks what you want to do with the file, select Move to Trash.

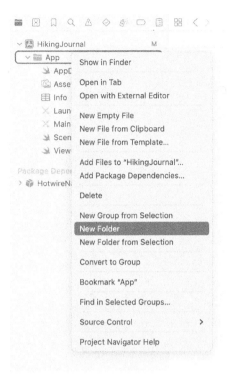

Your Project Navigator will now look like this:

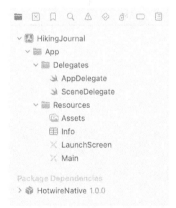

Now, try and run the app again.

We have a problem. This time, the error isn't even related to code. It's related to our configuration, as shown in the screenshot on page 64.

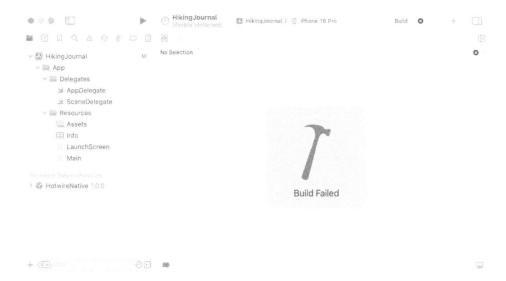

Inspect the error by opening the Issues navigator: click the exclamation point inside the gray triangle icon in the upper left, or press ⌘ 5. This shows all of the project's errors and warnings.

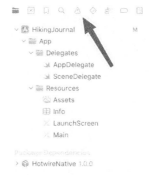

Click on the only issue to see the full error message. Xcode is trying to tell us that it can't find Info.plist in the old directory, HikingJournal. This makes sense since we moved this file to App/Resources, as shown in the screenshot on page 65.

Fix the issue by opening the Project Navigator again via ⌘ 1 and clicking the HikingJournal project at the top. Select HikingJournal from the list of *Targets* (not Project) in the middle column. Then select the Build Settings tab at the top.

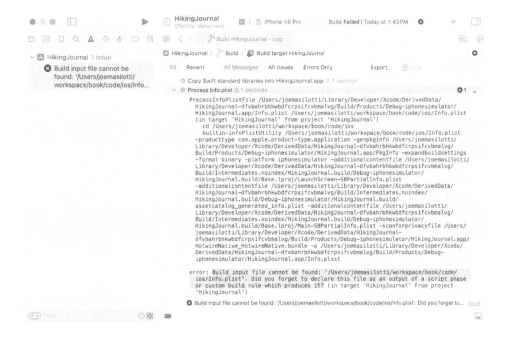

This is where you can configure all sorts of complicated settings related to how the app is built. We won't mess around with these settings very much in this book, but you do need to change one option here.

Search for "Info.plist File" in the upper right search box. Then change HikingJournal/Info.plist to the new location, App/Resources/Info.plist.

Now run the app again. Phew! The app is building, and the files are nicely tucked away in their respective folders. Now that you've cleaned up the iOS directories, you can configure the tabs.

Configure Tabs on iOS

Hotwire Native comes with first-party support for native tabs with HotwireTab-BarController. To configure the tabs for your app, you'll have to do the following:

1. Create a model to manage the tabs.
2. Migrate from Navigator to HotwireTabBarController.

Manage Tabs with a Model

You'll keep track of the individual tabs in a model object. It will be responsible for configuring each tab's visual appearance and which URL to display from the server. Having this configuration in one place also means we can update a single file to change our tabs.

Get started by creating a new folder under App named Models. Then right-click the Models folder and select New File From Template....

Select the iOS tab at the top and Swift File under the Source section, and click Next.

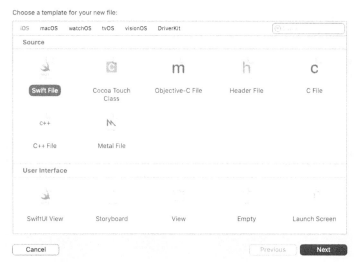

On the next screen, type "Tabs" in the Save As field at the top. Toward the bottom, make sure the Models folder is selected for Group and the HikingJournal target is checked. Click Create.

Xcode will automatically open the file for you. When it does, delete the generated contents and import the Hotwire and UIKit frameworks. Then, create two private HotwireTab variables, one for each link in the navigation bar: Hikes and Hikers.

ch04_02/ios/App/Models/Tabs.swift

```
import HotwireNative
import UIKit

private let hikesTab = HotwireTab(
    title: "Hikes",
    image: UIImage(systemName: "map")!,
    url: baseURL.appending(path: "hikes")
)

private let hikersTab = HotwireTab(
    title: "Hikers",
    image: UIImage(systemName: "figure.hiking")!,
    url: baseURL.appending(path: "users")
)
```

The strings passed to UIImage(systemName:) reference icons provided by SF Symbols,[1] a library from Apple that includes more than 5,000 symbols that you can freely use in iOS apps. I recommend downloading SF Symbols and digging through the plethora of options.

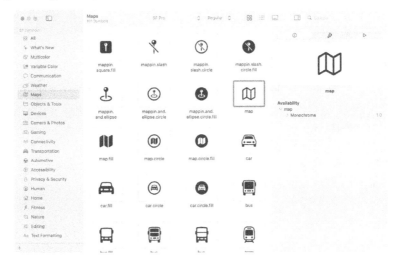

Next, *extend* HotwireTab to add a new static property: tabs. Extensions are like opening up classes or monkey patching in Ruby. They let us add functionality to classes, even ones we don't own like HotwireTab from Hotwire Native.

HotwireTab.all mimics the method of the same name from ActiveRecord, creating a nice parallel back to Rails.

---

1. https://developer.apple.com/sf-symbols/

ch04_03/ios/App/Models/Tabs.swift

```
import HotwireNative
import UIKit

private let hikesTab = HotwireTab(
    title: "Hikes",
    image: UIImage(systemName: "map")!,
    url: baseURL.appending(path: "hikes")
)

private let hikersTab = HotwireTab(
    title: "Hikers",
    image: UIImage(systemName: "figure.hiking")!,
    url: baseURL.appending(path: "users")
)

extension HotwireTab {
    static let all = [
        hikesTab,
        hikersTab
    ]
}
```

Our model is complete—we'll use these tabs to populate a tab bar controller.

Migrate from Navigator to HotwireTabBarController

Open SceneDelegate and replace the Navigator property with a HotwireTabBarController.

ch04_04/ios/App/Delegates/SceneDelegate.swift

```
import HotwireNative
import UIKit

let baseURL = URL(string: "http://localhost:3000")!

class SceneDelegate: UIResponder, UIWindowSceneDelegate {
    var window: UIWindow?

    private let tabBarController = HotwireTabBarController()

    func scene(
        _ scene: UIScene,
        willConnectTo session: UISceneSession,
        options connectionOptions: UIScene.ConnectionOptions
    ) {
        window?.rootViewController = navigator.rootViewController
        navigator.start()
    }
}
```

To get the tab bar controller on the screen, we need to assign it to the window. Assign the rootViewController to the HotwireTabBarController instance. Finally, load the tabs from our HotwireTab extension via load().

```
ch04_05/ios/App/Delegates/SceneDelegate.swift
import HotwireNative
import UIKit

let baseURL = URL(string: "http://localhost:3000")!

class SceneDelegate: UIResponder, UIWindowSceneDelegate {
    var window: UIWindow?

    private let tabBarController = HotwireTabBarController()

    func scene(
        _ scene: UIScene,
        willConnectTo session: UISceneSession,
        options connectionOptions: UIScene.ConnectionOptions
    ) {
        window?.rootViewController = tabBarController
        tabBarController.load(HotwireTab.all)
    }
}
```

Now the iOS app has a way to navigate between the pages we removed in the previous chapter when we hid the web-based navigation bar. And iOS users will immediately be more familiar with your app because you're using platform-specific, native controls.

The best part about this approach? Adding a *new* tab requires only a few lines of code. For example, if we had a new "Likes" route, we could add a tab for it like this to Tabs.swift:

```
// ...
private let likesTab = HotwireTab(
    title: "Likes",
    image: UIImage(systemName: "hand.thumbsup")!,
    url: baseURL.appending(path: "likes")
)

extension HotwireTab {
    static let all = [
        hikesTab,
        hikersTab,
        likesTab
    ]
}
```

That's all the Swift we need. Everything else for this new feature would exist in your Rails codebase. This is another example of where a tiny bit of native code in the right spot can elevate your app experience.

For Android, you'll start in the same way by organizing your code. Luckily, you only have one file, MainActivity.kt, so this will be quick.

Clean Up the Android Packages

Android uses *packages* to modularize and namespace code. When we created our app, we set the default package to com.masilotti.hikingjournal. Each package mirrors a directory on the file system, similar to how folders work in Xcode.

In Android Studio, create a new package by right-clicking com.masilotti.hikingjournal and selecting New and then Package.

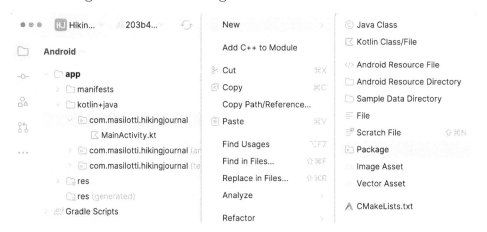

To match our naming conventions of the iOS app, inspired by Rails, name the package com.masilotti.hikingjournal.activities. Then drag MainActivity.kt inside the new package. Click OK in the dialog to automatically update any references to the file's new location.

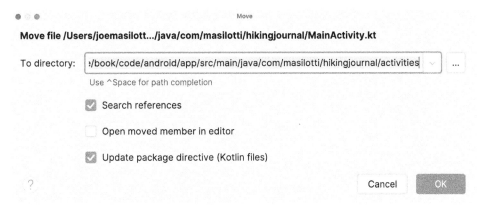

Configure Tabs on Android

With your Android directories in good shape, you can now configure the tabs. Here's how:

1. Update the layout XML for tabs.
2. Manage tabs with a model.
3. Initialize the tab bar.

Update the Layout XML for Tabs

Start by opening activity_main.xml. Here's a reminder of what that file looks like now:

```
ch04_07/android/app/src/main/res/layout/activity_main.xml
<?xml version="1.0" encoding="utf-8"?>
<androidx.fragment.app.FragmentContainerView
    xmlns:android="http://schemas.android.com/apk/res/android"
    xmlns:app="http://schemas.android.com/apk/res-auto"
    android:id="@+id/main"
    android:name="dev.hotwire.navigation.navigator.NavigatorHost"
    android:layout_width="match_parent"
    android:layout_height="match_parent"
    app:defaultNavHost="false" />
```

The layout renders a single node, a FragmentContainerView, for the web view. We need to render two web views (one for each tab) and the tab bar. But XML documents can only be comprised of a single root node.

Wrap the existing node in a ConstraintLayout element. This allows multiple child elements and gives us more control over how much height each node takes up on the screen.

ch04_08/android/app/src/main/res/layout/activity_main.xml
```xml
<?xml version="1.0" encoding="utf-8"?>
<androidx.constraintlayout.widget.ConstraintLayout
    xmlns:android="http://schemas.android.com/apk/res/android"
    xmlns:app="http://schemas.android.com/apk/res-auto"
    android:id="@+id/main"
    android:layout_width="match_parent"
    android:layout_height="match_parent">

    <androidx.fragment.app.FragmentContainerView
        android:id="@+id/hikes_nav_host"
        android:name="dev.hotwire.navigation.navigator.NavigatorHost"
        android:layout_width="match_parent"
        android:layout_height="match_parent"
        app:defaultNavHost="false" />

</androidx.constraintlayout.widget.ConstraintLayout>
```

Next, add a BottomNavigationView sibling node to render the tab view. We'll use the app:layout_constraint* properties to make sure it sticks to the bottom of the screen and fills the full width.

ch04_09/android/app/src/main/res/layout/activity_main.xml
```xml
<?xml version="1.0" encoding="utf-8"?>
<androidx.constraintlayout.widget.ConstraintLayout
    xmlns:android="http://schemas.android.com/apk/res/android"
    xmlns:app="http://schemas.android.com/apk/res-auto"
    android:id="@+id/main"
    android:layout_width="match_parent"
    android:layout_height="match_parent">

    <androidx.fragment.app.FragmentContainerView
        android:id="@+id/hikes_nav_host"
        android:name="dev.hotwire.navigation.navigator.NavigatorHost"
        android:layout_width="match_parent"
        android:layout_height="match_parent"
        app:defaultNavHost="false" />

➤   <com.google.android.material.bottomnavigation.BottomNavigationView
➤       android:id="@+id/bottom_nav"
➤       android:layout_width="match_parent"
➤       android:layout_height="wrap_content"
➤       app:labelVisibilityMode="labeled"
➤       app:layout_constraintBottom_toBottomOf="parent"
➤       app:layout_constraintEnd_toEndOf="parent"
➤       app:layout_constraintStart_toStartOf="parent" />

</androidx.constraintlayout.widget.ConstraintLayout>
```

To ensure the views don't overlap each other, constrain the bottom of the web view to sit up snugly against the top of the tab bar. Then, give the web view zero initial height so it can fill all the remaining available space.

ch04_10/android/app/src/main/res/layout/activity_main.xml

```
<androidx.constraintlayout.widget.ConstraintLayout
    xmlns:android="http://schemas.android.com/apk/res/android"
    xmlns:app="http://schemas.android.com/apk/res-auto"
    android:id="@+id/main"
    android:layout_width="match_parent"
    android:layout_height="match_parent">

    <androidx.fragment.app.FragmentContainerView
        android:id="@+id/hikes_nav_host"
        android:name="dev.hotwire.navigation.navigator.NavigatorHost"
        android:layout_width="match_parent"
        android:layout_height="0dp"
        app:defaultNavHost="false"
        app:layout_constraintBottom_toTopOf="@id/bottom_nav"
        app:layout_constraintTop_toTopOf="parent" />

    <!-- ... -->
</androidx.constraintlayout.widget.ConstraintLayout>
```

Add the second web view for the Hikers tab by copy-pasting another Fragment-ContainerView. Make sure to update the android:id property of each. Note how they read @+id/hikes_nav_host and @+id/hikers_nav_host, to better reflect the new layout. The other properties remain the same.

ch04_11/android/app/src/main/res/layout/activity_main.xml

```
<androidx.constraintlayout.widget.ConstraintLayout
    xmlns:android="http://schemas.android.com/apk/res/android"
    xmlns:app="http://schemas.android.com/apk/res-auto"
    android:id="@+id/main"
    android:layout_width="match_parent"
    android:layout_height="match_parent">

    <androidx.fragment.app.FragmentContainerView
        android:id="@+id/hikes_nav_host"
        android:name="dev.hotwire.navigation.navigator.NavigatorHost"
        android:layout_width="match_parent"
        android:layout_height="0dp"
        app:defaultNavHost="false"
        app:layout_constraintBottom_toTopOf="@id/bottom_nav"
        app:layout_constraintTop_toTopOf="parent" />

    <androidx.fragment.app.FragmentContainerView
        android:id="@+id/hikers_nav_host"
        android:name="dev.hotwire.navigation.navigator.NavigatorHost"
        android:layout_width="match_parent"
        android:layout_height="0dp"
        app:defaultNavHost="false"
        app:layout_constraintBottom_toTopOf="@id/bottom_nav"
        app:layout_constraintTop_toTopOf="parent" />

    <!-- ... -->
</androidx.constraintlayout.widget.ConstraintLayout>
```

You're all done with XML for now. Back to Kotlin.

Manage Tabs with a Model

Like on iOS, we'll use a model to represent each tab in the app. Start by creating a new package named com.masilotti.hikingjournal.models to hold your models.

Right-click the new package, select New, and then select Kotlin Class/File.

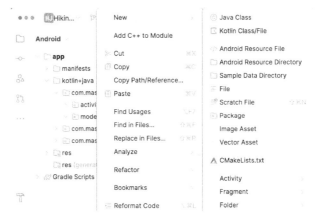

In the next dialog, enter "Tabs" for the name of the file, select File class, and hit Enter.

In this new file, create two private HotwireBottomTab variables, one for each link in the navigation bar. Set each navigatorHostId to match each FragmentContainerView via its android:id in the layout file.

ch04_12/android/app/src/main/java/com/masilotti/hikingjournal/models/Tabs.kt

```kotlin
package com.masilotti.hikingjournal.activities.models

import com.masilotti.hikingjournal.R
import com.masilotti.hikingjournal.activities.baseURL
import dev.hotwire.navigation.navigator.NavigatorConfiguration
import dev.hotwire.navigation.tabs.HotwireBottomTab

private val hikes = HotwireBottomTab(
    title = "Hikes",
```

```
        iconResId = android.R.drawable.ic_menu_mapmode,
        configuration = NavigatorConfiguration(
            name = "hikes",
            navigatorHostId = R.id.hikes_nav_host,
            startLocation = "$baseURL/hikes"
        )
    )
    private val hikers = HotwireBottomTab(
        title = "Hikers",
        iconResId = android.R.drawable.ic_menu_myplaces,
        configuration = NavigatorConfiguration(
            name = "hikers",
            navigatorHostId = R.id.hikers_nav_host,
            startLocation = "$baseURL/users"
        )
    )
)
```

These icons, prefaced with android.R.drawable, come from Android's built-in (but limited) asset library.[2]

Next, expose these new tabs in a list at the bottom of the file. We'll use this variable to configure the tabs back in MainActivity.

ch04_13/android/app/src/main/java/com/masilotti/hikingjournal/models/Tabs.kt
```
package com.masilotti.hikingjournal.activities.models

import com.masilotti.hikingjournal.R
import com.masilotti.hikingjournal.activities.baseURL
import dev.hotwire.navigation.navigator.NavigatorConfiguration
import dev.hotwire.navigation.tabs.HotwireBottomTab

private val hikes = HotwireBottomTab(
    // ...
)

private val hikers = HotwireBottomTab(
    // ...
)

val mainTabs = listOf(
    hikes,
    hikers
)
```

A heads up that in Kotlin, (almost) every new reference needs to be explicitly imported. But you don't need to do this manually. Let's say you forgot to import R in the previous code snippet. Hover over the red R and press ⌥ ↵, and then ↵ again to have Android Studio add the import statement for you, as shown in the screenshot on page 76.

---

2.   https://developer.android.com/reference/android/R.drawable

```
package com.masilotti.hikingjournal.activities.models

import com.masilotti.hikingjournal.activities.baseURL
import dev.hotwire.navigation.navigator.NavigatorConfiguration
import dev.hotwire.navigation.tabs.HotwireBottomTab

private val hikes = HotwireBottomTab(
    title = "Hikes",
    iconResId = android.R.drawable.ic_menu_mapmode,
    configuration = NavigatorConfiguration(
        name = "hikes",
        navigatorHostId = R.id.hikes_nav_host,
        startLocation = "$    Unresolved reference 'R'.
    )
                           Import    More actions...
)

private val hikers = HotwireBottomTab(
    title = "HIkers",
    iconResId = android.R.drawable.ic_menu_myplaces,
    configuration = NavigatorConfiguration(
        name = "hikers",
        navigatorHostId = R.id.hikers_nav_host,
        startLocation = "$baseURL/users"
    )
)
```

Moving forward, I won't mention any import statements. But I'll highlight any changes in the code snippets with arrows to make sure you don't forget them.

Android tab modeling is complete! Let's get the tabs on the screen.

Initialize the Tab Bar

Open MainActivity and create a private HotwireBottomNavigationController property. Declare it with lateinit so it can be created *after* the fragment is initialized.

ch04_14/android/app/src/main/java/com/masilotti/hikingjournal/activities/MainActivity.kt

```
// ...
import dev.hotwire.core.turbo.config.PathConfiguration
import dev.hotwire.navigation.activities.HotwireActivity
import dev.hotwire.navigation.navigator.NavigatorConfiguration
import dev.hotwire.navigation.tabs.HotwireBottomNavigationController
import dev.hotwire.navigation.util.applyDefaultImeWindowInsets

const val baseURL = "http://10.0.2.2:3000"

class MainActivity : HotwireActivity() {
    private lateinit var bottomNavigationController:
            HotwireBottomNavigationController

    override fun onCreate(savedInstanceState: Bundle?) {
        // ...
    }

    override fun navigatorConfigurations() = listOf(
        // ..
    )
}
```

Then, create a new private function at the bottom of MainActivity that initializes HotwireBottomNavigationController with a reference to our bottom navigation view. Call this function at the bottom of onCreate(savedInstanceState: Bundle?).

ch04_15/android/app/src/main/java/com/masilotti/hikingjournal/activities/MainActivity.kt
```kotlin
package com.masilotti.hikingjournal.activities

import android.os.Bundle
import android.view.View
import androidx.activity.enableEdgeToEdge
➤ import com.google.android.material.bottomnavigation.BottomNavigationView
import com.masilotti.hikingjournal.R
➤ import com.masilotti.hikingjournal.activities.models.mainTabs
import dev.hotwire.core.config.Hotwire
import dev.hotwire.core.turbo.config.PathConfiguration
import dev.hotwire.navigation.activities.HotwireActivity
import dev.hotwire.navigation.navigator.NavigatorConfiguration
import dev.hotwire.navigation.tabs.HotwireBottomNavigationController
import dev.hotwire.navigation.util.applyDefaultImeWindowInsets

const val baseURL = "http://10.0.2.2:3000"

class MainActivity : HotwireActivity() {
    private lateinit var bottomNavigationController:
            HotwireBottomNavigationController

    override fun onCreate(savedInstanceState: Bundle?) {
        // ...

➤        initializeBottomTabs()
    }

    override fun navigatorConfigurations() = listOf(
        // ..
    )

➤    private fun initializeBottomTabs() {
➤        val bottomNavigationView =
➤            findViewById<BottomNavigationView>(R.id.bottom_nav)
➤
➤        bottomNavigationController =
➤            HotwireBottomNavigationController(this, bottomNavigationView)
➤        bottomNavigationController.load(mainTabs, 0)
➤    }
}
```

The last line, bottomNavigationController.load(mainTabs, 0), loads the first tab on launch—the one at index 0.

Wrap everything up by using your tabs model to determine the navigator configurations. Replace the implementation of navigatorConfigurations() with mainTabs.navigatorConfigurations(). With this handy helper, Hotwire Native extends lists comprised of HotwireBottomTab instances, converting tabs to configurations.

ch04_16/android/app/src/main/java/com/masilotti/hikingjournal/activities/MainActivity.kt

```
// ...
import dev.hotwire.navigation.activities.HotwireActivity
import dev.hotwire.navigation.tabs.HotwireBottomNavigationController
➤ import dev.hotwire.navigation.tabs.navigatorConfigurations
import dev.hotwire.navigation.util.applyDefaultImeWindowInsets

const val baseURL = "http://10.0.2.2:3000"

class MainActivity : HotwireActivity() {
    private lateinit var bottomNavigationController:
            HotwireBottomNavigationController

    override fun onCreate(savedInstanceState: Bundle?) {
        // ...
    }

➤    override fun navigatorConfigurations() = mainTabs.navigatorConfigurations

    private fun initializeBottomTabs() {
        // ...
    }
}
```

Run the app. You've got tabs!

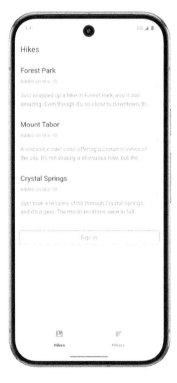

With that, you're back to feature parity with the iOS app. To get tabs working on Android, you had to update the XML layout to account for multiple fragments, model the tabs, and dynamically wire up a NavigatorConfiguration instance for each tab.

With more Kotlin written, you're building your confidence in creating mobile apps across multiple platforms. Nice work!

What's Next?

You just learned how to create and configure a native tab bar on iOS and Android. For iOS, you picked up some knowledge about SF Symbols. And on Android, you learned how to work with multiple views in a single XML layout.

When developing apps with Hotwire Native, simply being aware of first-party components like HotwireTabBarController and HotwireBottomNavigationController can often save a lot of time. I've gone through many iterations of custom versions of native tab bars, but I'll be sticking with the ones outlined in this chapter for a long time.

When it comes to interacting with native APIs in Hotwire Native apps, native tabs just scratch the surface. Next, we'll explore how to further level up our app with completely native screens powered by SwiftUI on iOS and then Jetpack Compose on Android.

## CHAPTER 5

Render Native Screens with SwiftUI

In the previous chapter, we added native tabs to swap between two web views and bring back our hidden web-based navigation links. But tabs are only a small portion of the screen, located all the way at the bottom. Sometimes we want to forgo the web entirely and render the entire UI with a more user-friendly, native implementation.

A major benefit of Hotwire Native is being able to do just this—to *drop down* into native Swift when needed. This unlocks access to the latest iOS APIs and provides developers with a way to render fully native screens.

In this chapter, you will learn how to decide which screens to upgrade to native vs. which are better rendered in the web view. Then, you'll build a native screen with SwiftUI in iOS.

There's a lot to cover when going native. So, to help keep the book flowing, I've split up the discussion of how to render native screens on iOS and Android between this chapter and the next one, Chapter 6, Render Native Screens with Jetpack Compose, on page 103.

Before we dive into SwiftUI code, let's first review *when* it makes sense to go fully native. Each native screen adds additional complexity and maintenance, so you'll want to reserve them for the highlights of your app.

When to Go Native

Going with a *native home screen* means the app can launch quickly and offer the highest fidelity possible right away. HEY and Basecamp both have fully native home screens, launching directly to SwiftUI or Jetpack Compose views. (Bonus: They cache the data for offline access, further speeding up launch times.)

37signals uses a native screen for each of the five tabs in their popular Basecamp app, as shown in the following image. These two iOS screens are fully native, not a single web-rendered element in sight!

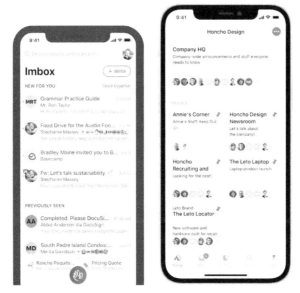

Native maps offer a better user experience than web-based solutions, as well. Gestures like swiping, pinching, and panning work as expected. And you can fill the entire screen with map tiles and tack on individual features as needed, like pins, overlays, or directions, as shown in the two screenshots on page 83.

Finally, screens that interact with *native APIs* are often easier to build directly in Swift and Kotlin. I recently worked on an app that displayed HealthKit and Google Health Platform data. By keeping everything native, the data flowed directly from the API to Swift and Kotlin. Trying to render this via HTML would have required multiple round trips via JavaScript, overcomplicating the process.

When to Keep Using the Web View

On the other hand, there are times when I recommend to continue rendering content from Rails code.

Screens that change frequently, like settings or preferences, are easier to manage when rendered via HTML. Changes on the web are cheap relative to native ones. A SwiftUI or Jetpack Compose update often requires updates to the view *and* the API on the server. And each API change needs to ensure backward compatibility with all previous versions.

The following screenshot shows a settings screen on the left and a checkout flow on the right. These screens change frequently, for example, adding a new profile field or a way to use coupon codes when checking out. It's best to keep these web-based so they require less code to write and maintain.

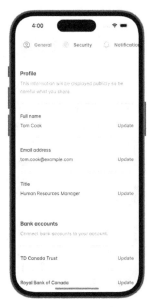

Boring *CRUD-like operations* that aren't unique to your app's experience or product probably don't need to be native. Yes, they might be fun to experiment with. But the time and resources spent are most likely better served when working on critical workflows like native home screens and maps or interacting heavily with native APIs.

Lastly, rendering *a lot of dynamic content* is often quicker to build on the web. If we went native, a list of heterogeneous items, like a news feed, requires each item type to be implemented as its own native view. And each *new* item type requires new releases to the app stores. Leaving all this logic and rendering to the server helps ensure the apps won't block new features on the web.

Now that we have a loose framework for deciding which screens to upgrade to native and which to keep as web views, can you think of anything in our app that could benefit from a native makeover?

Build a Native Screen with SwiftUI

For our Hiking Journal app, we're going to upgrade the web-based map screen to a native one powered by SwiftUI,[1] Apple's declarative framework for building user interfaces.

The next image is a before (left) and after (right) shot of what you'll build. It might not *look* much different, but interacting with the native map on the right will be a much better experience for your users. I mean, have you ever tried to pan or zoom a map on a mobile website? What a pain!

---

1. https://developer.apple.com/xcode/swiftui/

Adding our SwiftUI map screen to the Hotwire Native app requires a few steps:

1. Render a map with a SwiftUI view.
2. Connect the view to Hotwire Native with a view controller.
3. Route the URL via path configuration.
4. Expose a JSON endpoint for structured hike data.
5. Fetch and parse the JSON with a model and a view model.

Render a Map with a SwiftUI View

Your first step in upgrading the web-based map screen is to create a new SwiftUI view. Create a new folder under App named Views, and then create a new file. As the template for your new file, select SwiftUI View from the User Interface section. Name the file MapView.

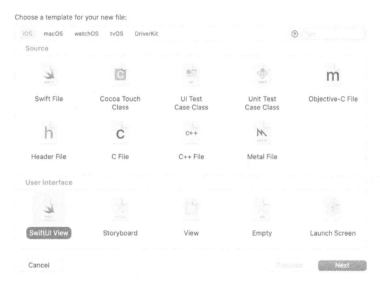

When the new file opens, you're presented with a new interface on the far right. This is the *Canvas Editor*, showing a SwiftUI preview pane. You can toggle between the right and left panes by clicking the Editor menu and then Assistant or by pressing ⌘ ⌥ ↵.

Launch the preview by clicking the Editor menu item, then Canvas, and then Refresh Canvas or ⌘ ⌥ P. You'll see the view rendered on the right, as shown in the screenshot on page 86.

The SwiftUI view renders whatever is inside the body property. Here, it is a Text() element saying "Hello, World!" Change the text and watch as the live preview updates automatically. Although this is a sign that your app is building successfully, you might need to refresh the canvas to get it started.

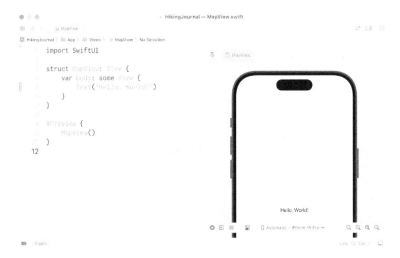

Anything inside that #Preview macro at the bottom gets rendered on the right, right now an instance of the new view you created, MapView.

At the top of the file, import the MapKit framework and replace the contents of body with a Map.

ch05_01/ios/App/Views/MapView.swift

```swift
import MapKit
import SwiftUI

struct MapView: View {
    var body: some View {
        Map {
        }
    }
}

#Preview {
    MapView()
}
```

Inside of Map, create a coordinate and pass it to a new Marker class. Here, I'm using the name and rough location of a local hike near where I live in Portland, OR—the beautiful Mount Tabor.

ch05_02/ios/App/Views/MapView.swift

```swift
struct MapView: View {
    var body: some View {
        Map {
            let coordinate = CLLocationCoordinate2D(
                latitude: 45.511881,
                longitude: -122.595706
            )
```

```
        Marker("Mount Tabor", coordinate: coordinate)
        }
    }
}
```

We can't directly render a SwiftUI view in the app just yet. We first need to wrap it in a view controller.

Connect to Hotwire Native with a View Controller

Under the Controllers folder, create a new Swift file named MapController. As usual, delete the contents. Then import both SwiftUI and UIKit.

Declare a MapController class but don't inherit from UIViewController. Instead, inherit from UIHostingController<MapView>.

ch05_03/ios/App/Controllers/MapController.swift
```
import SwiftUI
import UIKit

class MapController: UIHostingController<MapView> {
}
```

The UI framework we've been using up until now is called UIKit. Remember importing UIKit at the top of a few files in previous chapters? From experience, this framework aligns nicely with how Hotwire Native and Rails apps navigate between views. But our map view is built with SwiftUI, not UIKit. So we need a way to bridge the gap between the two frameworks.

UIHostingController[2] does exactly that. Each hosting controller needs to be *typed*—the class name between the angle brackets means that this controller renders a MapView.

Next, create a *convenience* initializer that accepts a URL. You'll use this later to determine which hike to render a map for. Inside the initializer, create a MapView and pass it to self.init(rootView:).

ch05_04/ios/App/Controllers/MapController.swift
```
import SwiftUI
import UIKit

class MapController: UIHostingController<MapView> {
    convenience init(url: URL) {
        let view = MapView()
        self.init(rootView: view)
    }
}
```

---

2. https://developer.apple.com/documentation/swiftui/uihostingcontroller

> ## Initializers in Swift
>
> In Swift, initializers are a bit like Rails model constructors, such as Model.new or custom methods you define to prepare objects before saving them to the database. Swift distinguishes between two types of initializers: *designated* and *convenience*.
>
> - *Designated initializers* are the primary entry points for creating instances of a class. Every class must have at least one designated initializer, which is responsible for fully initializing all the properties introduced by that class before calling the initializer of its superclass. Think of these as the "core" initializers.
>
> - *Convenience initializers*, on the other hand, are secondary helpers that make creating instances easier or more flexible. They're like Rails scopes or helper methods that simplify certain use cases without replacing the underlying logic. Convenience initializers call a designated initializer within the same class, often adding some extra processing or providing a shorthand for common configurations.
>
> To tie it back to Rails: a *designated initializer* is like defining initialize in a Ruby class, while a *convenience initializer* is like writing a self.create_from_url(url)' class method to handle a specific use case.

Route the URL via Path Configuration

As we learned in Chapter 3, Navigate Gracefully with Path Configuration, on page 47, our path configuration helps us keep our business logic on the server. This creates low-maintenance, server-driven apps. In our scenario here, instead of hard-coding which URL paths to render as maps, we can apply path properties from our remote JSON file.

Start by adding a new rule to the path configuration on the server, matching the path for a hike's map to assign the view_controller property.

ch05_05/rails/app/controllers/configurations_controller.rb
```
class ConfigurationsController < ApplicationController
  def ios_v1
    render json: {
      settings: {},
      rules: [
        {
          patterns: [
            "/new$",
            "/edit$"
          ],
          properties: {
            context: "modal"
          }
        },
        {
```

```
          patterns: [
            "/hikes/[0-9]+/map"
          ],
          properties: {
            view_controller: "map"
          }
        }
      ]
    }
  end

  def android_v1
    # ...
  end
end
```

Like context, Hotwire Native iOS is aware of the view_controller property, too. The framework exposes it when the user taps a new link via the NavigatorDelegate. As a quick refresher from Chapter 1, Build Your First Hotwire Native Apps, on page 1, *delegates* are a design pattern in iOS. They provide a way for objects to act on behalf of others to handle specific events, like when a link is tapped.

Our SceneDelegate is the one creating the Navigators via HotwireTabBarController, so that's a great place to implement NavigatorDelgate. At the bottom of SceneDelegate.swift, add an extension that implements the NavigatorDelegate protocol and implements this function.

ch05_06/ios/App/Delegates/SceneDelegate.swift
```
import HotwireNative
import UIKit

let baseURL = URL(string: "http://localhost:3000")!

class SceneDelegate: UIResponder, UIWindowSceneDelegate {
    // ...
}

extension SceneDelegate: NavigatorDelegate {
    func handle(
        proposal: VisitProposal,
        from navigator: Navigator
    ) -> ProposalResult {
    }
}
```

handle(proposal:) is called every time the user taps a link. It gives us an opportunity to customize what type of screen is rendered. To do that, the function requires us to return a ProposalResult.

⌘-click ProposalResult to jump to the definition. (This is a handy way of navigating around code in Xcode.) Here's what the contents of ProposalResult.swift show:

```swift
// hotwire-native-ios:Source/Turbo/Navigator/Helpers/ProposalResult.swift

import UIKit

/// Return from `NavigatorDelegate.handle(proposal:)` to route a custom controller.
public enum ProposalResult: Equatable {
    /// Route a `VisitableViewController`.
    case accept

    /// Route a custom `UIViewController` or subclass
    case acceptCustom(UIViewController)

    /// Do not route. Navigation is not modified.
    case reject
}
```

The ProposalResult class is an *enumeration*, which means it defines common types for a group of related values and enables you to work with them in a type-safe way.

The three cases are used like so:

- .accept—Route a web view for rendering web content.
- .acceptCustom—Route a custom view controller.
- .reject—Cancel and ignore the proposal.

We'll use the .acceptCustom case and pass in our fancy new MapController class for map routes.

```swift
// ch05_07/ios/App/Delegates/SceneDelegate.swift
import HotwireNative
import UIKit

let baseURL = URL(string: "http://localhost:3000")!

class SceneDelegate: UIResponder, UIWindowSceneDelegate {
    // ...
}

extension SceneDelegate: NavigatorDelegate {
    func handle(
        proposal: VisitProposal,
        from navigator: Navigator
    ) -> ProposalResult {
        switch proposal.viewController {
        case "map": .acceptCustom(MapController(url: proposal.url))
        }
    }
}
```

And for everything else, .accept will render the default web view provided by Hotwire Native.

ch05_08/ios/App/Delegates/SceneDelegate.swift
```
import HotwireNative
import UIKit

let baseURL = URL(string: "http://localhost:3000")!

class SceneDelegate: UIResponder, UIWindowSceneDelegate {
    // ...
}

extension SceneDelegate: NavigatorDelegate {
    func handle(
        proposal: VisitProposal,
        from navigator: Navigator
    ) -> ProposalResult {
        switch proposal.viewController {
        case "map": .acceptCustom(MapController(url: proposal.url))
        default: .accept
        }
    }
}
```

Wrap up the routing by assigning self to the navigator delegate of the HotwireTabBarController instance. We also need to change let to lazy var since this now depends on SceneDelegate being created via the reference to self, just like lateinit in Initialize the Tab Bar, on page 76.

ch05_09/ios/App/Delegates/SceneDelegate.swift
```
import HotwireNative
import UIKit

let baseURL = URL(string: "http://localhost:3000")!

class SceneDelegate: UIResponder, UIWindowSceneDelegate {
    var window: UIWindow?

    private lazy var tabBarController = HotwireTabBarController(
        navigatorDelegate: self
    )
    // ...
}

extension SceneDelegate: NavigatorDelegate {
    // ...
}
```

Run the app and navigate to a hike page. When you tap the Map button, you'll see a native map, as shown in the screenshot on page 92.

We'll address the satellite view a bit later. But for now, take a second to learn how to manipulate the map in the simulator. This will give you a good idea of how much better the user experience is compared to a web-based map.

Manipulating the Map

In the simulator, you can hold down the ⌥ key to create a second "finger," which is useful for zooming in and out on the map. You can then hold down ⇧ to "stick" them together for two-finger scrolls.

Expose a JSON Endpoint for Structured Hike Data

Our native map is now rendering beautifully and routing at the right time. But it still hardcodes the marker's name and coordinate, which isn't useful. Let's change that by dynamically pulling in data based on the hike.

Back in the Rails app, create a new view at app/views/maps/show.json.jbuilder. This view will render whenever we hit /hikes/:id/map.json. With the help of Jbuilder, we can extract the hike's coordinates in a single line of code:

ch05_10/rails/app/views/maps/show.json.jbuilder
```
json.extract! @hike, :name, :latitude, :longitude
```

Go ahead and visit http://localhost:3000/hikes/1/map.json in your browser, and you'll see the following JSON response:

```
{
  "name":"Crystal Springs",
  "latitude":45.479588,
  "longitude":-122.635317
}
```

Fetch and Parse JSON with a Model and a View Model

To make it easier to work with dynamic data, we can decode the JSON response into a concrete model. With the help of Decodable, you can parse this JSON with a single line of code.

Create a Model

Create a new Swift file in the Models folder and name it Hike. Inside, create a new struct with the properties from the JSON payload, conforming to the Decodable protocol.

ch05_11/ios/App/Models/Hike.swift
```
struct Hike: Decodable {
    let name: String
    let latitude: Double
    let longitude: Double
}
```

Remember how Marker in the view required a coordinate? To do this, create a computed property for Hike that exposes the latitude and longitude as a CLLocationCoordinate2D. Make sure to import the MapKit framework at the top, too:

ch05_12/ios/App/Models/Hike.swift
```
➤ import MapKit

struct Hike: Decodable {
    let name: String
    let latitude: Double
    let longitude: Double

➤    var coordinate: CLLocationCoordinate2D {
➤        CLLocationCoordinate2D(
➤            latitude: latitude,
➤            longitude: longitude
➤        )
➤    }
}
```

With the model in place, you need somewhere to kick off your network request and populate the view. In SwiftUI, these places are usually called *view models*—they bind data to UI elements and perform some work to get them loaded into the app.

Create a View Model

Unlike MVC in Rails, SwiftUI uses the MVVM pattern to coordinate code. MVVM stands for Model, View, View Model, and consists of the following:

- Models—The data objects, similar to a Rails model
- Views—Render content to the screen, similar to a Rails view
- View models—Coordinate data flow between the two, like a Rails controller

The view model you create for the app will be responsible for three things:

1. Building a URL to fetch the JSON
2. Fetching the JSON from the network
3. Parsing the JSON into a model

First, create a new folder named ViewModels and add a Swift file named HikeViewModel to it. Inside, delete the comments but leave the import statement. Declare a class to match the filename and add the @Observable keyword before it, like so:

ch05_13/ios/App/ViewModels/HikeViewModel.swift
```
import Foundation

@Observable class HikeViewModel {
}
```

The @Observable macro binds public properties to the view it's attached to. Changes trigger a redraw of the view, automatically updating the screen with the latest information, all without manually adding any callbacks or hooks.

Add a public, optional Hike property:

ch05_14/ios/App/ViewModels/HikeViewModel.swift
```
import Foundation

@Observable class HikeViewModel {
    var hike: Hike?
}
```

Now, any time the hike changes, the view will automatically be redrawn!

@Observable Macro

The @Observable macro is powerful. But note that it requires iOS 17. If you're targeting older versions of iOS, then you'll need to use the ObservedObject protocol and @Published property wrapper to achieve the same result.

More information on the three properties can be found in Apple's migration guide.[3]

Build the URL to Fetch the JSON

Now, add a private property to hold the URL and, in the initializer, append the JSON path extension:

ch05_15/ios/App/ViewModels/HikeViewModel.swift
```
import Foundation

@Observable class HikeViewModel {
    var hike: Hike?

➤    private let url: URL
➤
➤    init(url: URL) {
➤        self.url = url.appendingPathExtension("json")
➤    }
}
```

You need to append JSON because the original navigation was triggered via the web, to /hikes/:id/map. With .json at the end, the server will know to serve the Jbuilder view you created earlier.

Fetch the JSON from the Network

Create a new function to fetch the JSON, using the shared URLSession to make the network request:

ch05_16/ios/App/ViewModels/HikeViewModel.swift
```
import Foundation

@Observable class HikeViewModel {
    var hike: Hike?

    private let url: URL

    init(url: URL) {
        self.url = url.appendingPathExtension("json")
    }
```

---

3.   https://developer.apple.com/documentation/swiftui/migrating-from-the-observable-object-protocol-to-the-observable-macro

```
func fetchCoordinates() async {
    do {
        let (data, _) = try await URLSession.shared.data(from: url)
    } catch {
        print("Failed to fetch hike: \(error.localizedDescription)")
    }
}
}
```

There are a few new concepts going on here, so let's break them down:

- Asynchronous code—From the top, the async keyword allows this function to call asynchronous code. We need the await keyword when calling data(from:) to break out of the current thread and return asynchronously. This differs from Ruby, where most code is *blocking* - calling Ruby code that makes an HTTP request will "wait" until it returns. In Swift, we have to be a bit more explicit.

- Error handling—do, try, and catch are Swift's approach to error handling. Functions that can raise errors must be called with the try keyword. And anything that calls these functions must be wrapped in a do/catch block. catch handles any errors that arise, automatically exposing the error that occurred. These map pretty closely to begin and rescue in Ruby.

- Ignored variables—data(from:) returns a tuple with a reference to the data and HTTP response. We only care about the data, so we can use an underscore to ignore the other element, just like in Ruby.

Parse the JSON and Create a Hike

Use a JSONDecoder to decode the JSON response directly into a Hike instance. This call can also raise an error, so don't forget the try keyword:

ch05_17/ios/App/ViewModels/HikeViewModel.swift
```
import Foundation

@Observable class HikeViewModel {
    var hike: Hike?

    private let url: URL

    init(url: URL) {
        self.url = url.appendingPathExtension("json")
    }

    func fetchCoordinates() async {
        do {
            let (data, _) = try await URLSession.shared.data(from: url)
            hike = try JSONDecoder().decode(Hike.self, from: data)
        } catch {
```

```
        print("Failed to fetch hike: \(error.localizedDescription)")
        }
    }
}
```

Here, hike refers to the property of HikeViewModel. Because HikeViewModel is an @Observable class, updating one of its properties informs SwiftUI to redraw the view—no additional code required.

Render the Dynamic Hike Data in the View

You now have code that fetches dynamic JSON from the server to create an instance of the Hike model. But none of these changes are being applied to the view yet. Let's address this.

Back in MapView.swift, add a property for the view model:

ch05_18/ios/App/Views/MapView.swift
```
struct MapView: View {
    var viewModel: HikeViewModel

    var body: some View {
        Map {
            let coordinate = CLLocationCoordinate2D(
                latitude: 45.511881,
                longitude: -122.595706
            )
            Marker("Mount Tabor", coordinate: coordinate)
        }
    }
}
```

We now have a property without a default value. Every time this view is created, we need to pass in a HikeViewModel instance. Address the preview in the same file first:

ch05_18/ios/App/Views/MapView.swift
```
#Preview {
    let url = URL(string: "https://example.com")!
    let viewModel = HikeViewModel(url: url)
    viewModel.hike = Hike(
        name: "Mount Tabor",
        latitude: 45.511881,
        longitude: -122.595706
    )
    return MapView(viewModel: viewModel)
}
```

We've passed in a dummy URL and reused the hardcoded name and coordinates from earlier. Note that the return keyword is now needed because #Preview is more than a single line of code. Try and run the project again.

Ugh, now Xcode is complaining somewhere else! Follow the build error by pressing ⌘ ' to navigate to MapController.

To fix this, like earlier, MapView needs an instance of the view model:

ch05_18/ios/App/Controllers/MapController.swift
```
import SwiftUI
import UIKit

class MapController: UIHostingController<MapView> {
    convenience init(url: URL) {
        let viewModel = HikeViewModel(url: url)
        let view = MapView(viewModel: viewModel)
        self.init(rootView: view)
    }
}
```

The project is building again, and Xcode is happy. Up next, you'll use the view model in the view to render the marker on the map.

Open MapView.swift and unwrap hike from the view model:

ch05_19/ios/App/Views/MapView.swift
```
struct MapView: View {
    var viewModel: HikeViewModel

    var body: some View {
        Map {
            if let hike = viewModel.hike {
                Marker(hike.name, coordinate: hike.coordinate)
            }
        }
    }
}
```

Run the app and check out the awesome, dynamic map of the...entire country, as shown in the screenshot on page 99.

Huh? Any idea what's going on?

We haven't actually called the fetchCoordinates() function from the view model we just created!

Fix this by adding a task to the Map, like so:

ch05_20/ios/App/Views/MapView.swift

```swift
struct MapView: View {
    var viewModel: HikeViewModel

    var body: some View {
        Map {
            if let hike = viewModel.hike {
                Marker(hike.name, coordinate: hike.coordinate)
            }
        }
        .task {
            await viewModel.fetchCoordinates()
        }
    }
}
```

.task() is a *modifier*, a way to apply changes to the view's appearance, behavior, or other properties—these are used extensively throughout SwiftUI. Here, the modifier runs whatever code is inside the curly braces when the view loads. Some modifiers add functionality like .task(), while others can change the way a view is rendered, like changing the background color with .background().

Run the app and visit the map again. It now renders each hike's coordinates and name dynamically.

You now have a map with all the touch, drag, and swipe affordances expected from a native app…but I think we can make it look even better.

Back in MapView.swift, add these Map modifiers to render a map that doesn't bleed into the navigation or tab bar and looks way more realistic:

```
ch05_21/ios/App/Views/MapView.swift
struct MapView: View {
    var viewModel: HikeViewModel

    var body: some View {
        Map {
            if let hike = viewModel.hike {
                Marker(hike.name, coordinate: hike.coordinate)
            }
        }
        .mapStyle(.hybrid(elevation: .realistic))
        .navigationTitle("Map")
        .clipped()
        .task {
            await viewModel.fetchCoordinates()
        }
    }
}
```

This gives us a beautiful rendering, as shown in the screenshot on page 101, which is much better than what we had before on the web.

And now, you have a dynamic map on iOS!

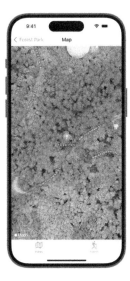

As you just learned, integrating a native screen requires a bit of coordination. First, you created a SwiftUI view that gets rendered via a UIHostingController. Then, you set the view_controller property in your path configuration to tell the client when to display the view controller. Following MVVM, you then created a model and a view model to fetch JSON data from the server to pass it to the map view. Finally, you wired everything up with a .task() modifier in the SwiftUI view to initiate the network request.

What's Next?

Building on this knowledge, you can build any native screen or interaction you want! You could swap out the map and render HealthKit data. Or convert the list of hikes to native elements and cache it for offline access. The list goes on.

But with every new native feature, it's important to understand the trade-offs. SwiftUI screens and the coordinating code are much more expensive to build and maintain. And as we reviewed earlier, they should only be reserved for the most critical pieces of your app.

Up next, we'll tackle the Android side of this—rendering a native screen with Jetpack Compose. But if you're all in on iOS right now, feel free to skip the next chapter and jump right to Chapter 7, Build iOS Bridge Components with Swift, on page 127. There, we'll upgrade individual *components* to native, without committing to an entire SwiftUI screen.

## CHAPTER 6

Render Native Screens with Jetpack Compose

In the previous chapter, we covered *when* to upgrade to native screens. Native home screens, native maps, and native API integration are all great candidates for going native. Whereas screens that change frequently, deal with CRUD-like operations, or render lots of dynamic content are better suited for an HTML-based approach. Feel free to review When to Go Native, on page 81, for a refresher.

This chapter focuses entirely on the Android side of things. We'll walk through converting our web-based map screen to one driven by a native Google Maps integration.

Integrate Jetpack Compose with Hotwire Native

We'll convert our web-based map on Android using Jetpack Compose,[1] Android's declarative UI framework. We'll follow an approach similar to that used with iOS, but with a few extra configuration steps:

1. Build a Jetpack Compose screen.
2. Route the URL via path configuration.
3. Configure Google Maps with an API key.
4. Add a map to the view.
5. Fetch and parse the JSON with a model and a view model.

Before we dive in, there's one step of cleanup. Remember how we configured Hotwire Native in MainActivity in Update the Activity, on page 21. On Android, we can put this Kotlin-powered configuration into a subclass of Application.

---

1. https://developer.android.com/compose

This code runs when the app is launched—perfect for setting up Hotwire Native.

First, next to the activities and models packages, create a new Kotlin file named HikingJournalApplication.kt that subclasses Application.

ch06_01/android/app/src/main/java/com/masilotti/hikingjournal/HikingJournalApplication.kt
```
package com.masilotti.hikingjournal

import android.app.Application

class HikingJournalApplication : Application() {
    override fun onCreate() {
        super.onCreate()
    }
}
```

Tell Android where this lives by setting android:name in AndroidManifest.xml. Note the leading dot!

ch06_02/android/app/src/main/AndroidManifest.xml
```
<manifest xmlns:android="http://schemas.android.com/apk/res/android"
    xmlns:tools="http://schemas.android.com/tools">

    <uses-permission android:name="android.permission.INTERNET" />

    <application
        android:name=".HikingJournalApplication"
        android:allowBackup="true"
        android:dataExtractionRules="@xml/data_extraction_rules"
        android:fullBackupContent="@xml/backup_rules"
        android:icon="@mipmap/ic_launcher"
        android:label="@string/app_name"
        android:roundIcon="@mipmap/ic_launcher_round"
        android:supportsRtl="true"
        android:theme="@style/Theme.HikingJournal"
        android:usesCleartextTraffic="true"
        tools:targetApi="31">

        <!-- ... -->
    </application>

</manifest>
```

Now, we can move the Hotwire Native code that loads our path configuration from MainActivity to the Application subclass.

ch06_02/android/app/src/main/java/com/masilotti/hikingjournal/HikingJournalApplication.kt
```
package com.masilotti.hikingjournal

import android.app.Application
import com.masilotti.hikingjournal.activities.baseURL
import dev.hotwire.core.config.Hotwire
import dev.hotwire.core.turbo.config.PathConfiguration
```

```
class HikingJournalApplication : Application() {
    override fun onCreate() {
        super.onCreate()

        Hotwire.loadPathConfiguration(
            context = this,
            location = PathConfiguration.Location(
                remoteFileUrl = "$baseURL/configurations/android_v1.json"
            )
        )
    }
}
```

We'll add more to this file later in the chapter. But for now, let's create the screen that will power the map.

Build a Jetpack Compose Screen

To work with Compose, we need to first update our project's configuration. Android Studio is integrated tightly with editing Compose files, so there are a few steps to make sure everything works.

Configure Compose

First, open libs.versions.toml under the Gradle Scripts directory and make sure Kotlin is set to 2.0.0 or later. This ensures we don't have to manually check Compose to Kotlin compatibility.[2]

```
[versions]
# ...
kotlin = "2.x.x"
# ...

[libraries]
# ...

[plugins]
# ...
```

In the same file, add the Compose Compiler plugin by adding compose-compiler = { id = "org.jetbrains.kotlin.plugin.compose", version.ref = "kotlin" } to the very bottom of the file, under the [plugins] section. Using version.ref = "kotlin" ensures that we always align the plugin's version with our version of Kotlin.

Apply the plugin in the *project's* build.gradle.kts (the *first* one under Gradle Scripts).

---

2. https://developer.android.com/jetpack/androidx/releases/compose-kotlin

ch06_05/android/build.gradle.kts
```
// Top-level build file where you can add configuration options common to all
// sub-projects/modules.
plugins {
    alias(libs.plugins.android.application) apply false
    alias(libs.plugins.kotlin.android) apply false
    alias(libs.plugins.compose.compiler) apply false
}
```

Then, open the *app's* build.gradle.kts (the *second* one). At the top, apply the plugin.

ch06_06/android/app/build.gradle.kts
```
plugins {
    alias(libs.plugins.android.application)
    alias(libs.plugins.kotlin.android)
    alias(libs.plugins.compose.compiler)
}
// ...
```

And enable Compose.

ch06_07/android/app/build.gradle.kts
```
// ...

android {
    // ...

    kotlinOptions {
        jvmTarget = "17"
    }

    buildFeatures {
        compose = true
    }
}

// ...
```

Finally, add the Jetpack Compose dependencies to the bottom of the same file. This mix gives us a nice baseline of UI elements and enables live previews in Android Studio.

ch06_08/android/app/build.gradle.kts
```
// ...

dependencies {
    implementation(libs.androidx.core.ktx)
    implementation(libs.androidx.appcompat)
    implementation(libs.material)
    implementation(libs.androidx.activity)
    implementation(libs.androidx.constraintlayout)
    implementation("dev.hotwire:core:1.2.0")
```

```
    implementation("dev.hotwire:navigation-fragments:1.2.0")
➤   implementation(platform("androidx.compose:compose-bom:2025.04.01"))
➤   implementation("androidx.compose.material3:material3")
➤   implementation("androidx.compose.ui:ui-tooling-preview")
➤   debugImplementation("androidx.compose.ui:ui-tooling")
    testImplementation(libs.junit)
    androidTestImplementation(libs.androidx.junit)
    androidTestImplementation(libs.androidx.espresso.core)
}
```

Make sure to sync Gradle after making all of your changes.

And with Compose added and configured, we can now create our view. But to render a view, we first need a fragment for it to be contained in.

Build a Compose View

Create a new package named fragments under com.masilotti.hikingjournal. Right-click the new package and navigate to New → Fragment → Fragment (Blank). Name the fragment MapFragment and click Finish. The wizard will create the Kotlin file and the XML layout to render a fragment.

Open the XML layout, fragment_map.xml, and replace the contents with a ComposeView wrapped in a ConstraintLayout, as follows. This will fill the entire screen with a view where we can attach Compose elements.

ch06_09/android/app/src/main/res/layout/fragment_map.xml
```xml
<?xml version="1.0" encoding="utf-8"?>
<androidx.constraintlayout.widget.ConstraintLayout
    xmlns:android="http://schemas.android.com/apk/res/android"
    xmlns:app="http://schemas.android.com/apk/res-auto"
    android:layout_width="match_parent"
    android:layout_height="match_parent">

    <androidx.compose.ui.platform.ComposeView
        android:id="@+id/compose_view"
        android:layout_width="match_parent"
        android:layout_height="match_parent" />

</androidx.constraintlayout.widget.ConstraintLayout>
```

In the newly created MapFragment.kt, replace the contents with an empty subclass of a HotwireFragment. This subclass wires us up to Hotwire Native, exposing a Navigator instance, which we'll use later in the chapter.

ch06_09/android/app/src/main/java/com/masilotti/hikingjournal/fragments/MapFragment.kt
```kotlin
package com.masilotti.hikingjournal.fragments

import dev.hotwire.navigation.fragments.HotwireFragment

class MapFragment : HotwireFragment() {
}
```

Override onCreateView() in the fragment to render our custom ComposeView by inflating it via R. Remember, R exposes our project's non-code resources.

ch06_10/android/app/src/main/java/com/masilotti/hikingjournal/fragments/MapFragment.kt

```
package com.masilotti.hikingjournal.fragments

➤ import android.os.Bundle
➤ import android.view.LayoutInflater
➤ import android.view.View
➤ import android.view.ViewGroup
➤ import com.masilotti.hikingjournal.R
  import dev.hotwire.navigation.fragments.HotwireFragment

  class MapFragment : HotwireFragment() {
➤     override fun onCreateView(
➤         inflater: LayoutInflater,
➤         container: ViewGroup?,
➤         savedInstanceState: Bundle?
➤     ): View {
➤         val view = inflater.inflate(R.layout.fragment_map, container, false)
➤         return view
➤     }
  }
```

Then, find the ComposeView in view and apply setContent(), bridging the gap to Compose. Inside, render a Text() node with the traditional "Hello, World!" string.

ch06_11/android/app/src/main/java/com/masilotti/hikingjournal/fragments/MapFragment.kt

```
  // ...
  import android.view.ViewGroup
➤ import androidx.compose.material3.Text
➤ import androidx.compose.ui.platform.ComposeView
  import com.masilotti.hikingjournal.R
  import dev.hotwire.navigation.fragments.HotwireFragment

  class MapFragment : HotwireFragment() {
      override fun onCreateView(
          inflater: LayoutInflater,
          container: ViewGroup?,
          savedInstanceState: Bundle?
      ): View {
          val view = inflater.inflate(R.layout.fragment_map, container, false)
➤         view.findViewById<ComposeView>(R.id.compose_view).apply {
➤             setContent {
➤                 Text(text = "Hello, World!")
➤             }
➤         }
          return view
      }
  }
```

Our Compose code will get a bit lengthy, so we don't want to keep it all inside of onCreateView(). Let's extract it to a standalone function at the bottom of the file, decorated with @Composable.

ch06_12/android/app/src/main/java/com/masilotti/hikingjournal/fragments/MapFragment.kt

```kotlin
// ...
import androidx.compose.material3.Text
➤ import androidx.compose.runtime.Composable
import androidx.compose.ui.platform.ComposeView
// ...

class MapFragment : HotwireFragment() {
    override fun onCreateView(
        inflater: LayoutInflater,
        container: ViewGroup?,
        savedInstanceState: Bundle?
    ): View {
        val view = inflater.inflate(R.layout.fragment_map, container, false)
        view.findViewById<ComposeView>(R.id.compose_view).apply {
            setContent {
➤               MapView()
            }
        }
        return view
    }
}

➤ @Composable
➤ fun MapView() {
➤     Text(text = "Hello, World!")
➤ }
```

Finally, decorate the new Compose function with @Preview to render a live preview in Android Studio.

ch06_13/android/app/src/main/java/com/masilotti/hikingjournal/fragments/MapFragment.kt

```kotlin
// ...
import androidx.compose.ui.platform.ComposeView
➤ import androidx.compose.ui.tooling.preview.Preview
import com.masilotti.hikingjournal.R
import dev.hotwire.navigation.fragments.HotwireFragment

class MapFragment : HotwireFragment() {
    // ...
}

➤ @Preview
@Composable
fun MapView() {
    Text(text = "Hello, World!")
}
```

Click the Split button in the upper right to view the live preview on the right side of the screen. Look at that, Jetpack Compose!

We now have a native screen powered by Jetpack Compose! But...there's no way to actually navigate to it. Up next, we'll expose the fragment to Hotwire Native and route the map URL as we did on iOS.

Route the URL via Path Configuration

Before we can navigate to the new fragment, MapFragment, we have to make Hotwire Native aware of it. In HikingJournalApplication.kt, register this and the default HotwireWebFragment with the framework.

ch06_14/android/app/src/main/java/com/masilotti/hikingjournal/HikingJournalApplication.kt

```
package com.masilotti.hikingjournal

import android.app.Application
import com.masilotti.hikingjournal.activities.baseURL
import com.masilotti.hikingjournal.fragments.MapFragment
import dev.hotwire.core.config.Hotwire
import dev.hotwire.core.turbo.config.PathConfiguration
import dev.hotwire.navigation.config.registerFragmentDestinations
import dev.hotwire.navigation.fragments.HotwireWebFragment

class HikingJournalApplication : Application() {
    override fun onCreate() {
        super.onCreate()

        Hotwire.loadPathConfiguration(
            context = this,
            location = PathConfiguration.Location(
                remoteFileUrl = "$baseURL/configurations/android_v1.json"
            )
        )

        Hotwire.registerFragmentDestinations(
```

```
➤          HotwireWebFragment::class,
➤          MapFragment::class,
➤      )
    }
}
```

Then, open MapFragment.kt and decorate the class with @HotwireDestinationDeepLink.
We'll use this URI in the path configuration to connect routes with this fragment. Hotwire Native uses this decoration to know which URIs correspond
to which fragments.

ch06_14/android/app/src/main/java/com/masilotti/hikingjournal/fragments/MapFragment.kt
```
// ...
import com.masilotti.hikingjournal.R
➤ import dev.hotwire.navigation.destinations.HotwireDestinationDeepLink
import dev.hotwire.navigation.fragments.HotwireFragment

➤ @HotwireDestinationDeepLink(uri = "hotwire://fragment/map")
class MapFragment : HotwireFragment() {
    // ...
}

// ...
```

In the Rails app, open configurations_controller.rb and add a new entry to the
#android_v1 method. We'll match the same pattern as we did on iOS, all "hike
map" paths, to set the uri property to what we just added to the fragment.

ch06_14/rails/app/controllers/configurations_controller.rb
```
class ConfigurationsController < ApplicationController
  def ios_v1
    # ...
  end

  def android_v1
    render json: {
      settings: {},
      rules: [
        # ...
➤       {
➤         patterns: [
➤           "/hikes/[0-9]+/map"
➤         ],
➤         properties: {
➤           uri: "hotwire://fragment/map",
➤           title: "Map"
➤         }
➤       }
      ]
    }
  end
end
```

Now, Hotwire Native knows *where* to send these URL paths: the fragment decorated with the matching @HotwireDestinationDeepLink, MapFragment.

Excellent! Run the app and click the Map button on any hike. You'll see the cute little "Hello, World!" text snuggled up to the top left of the screen.

Adorable? Yes. Useful? Not so much. Also, where'd the bar at the top of the screen go? How are we supposed to navigate back without a back button? Turns out, ComposeView takes over the *entire* screen. We need to manually add back in the toolbar at the top.

Open the layout file for this fragment, fragment_map.xml, and add an AppBarLayout with a MaterialToolbar inside of it. Then constrain the existing ComposeView so it sits right below. Also, enable android:fitsSystemWindows on the root element to make sure the screen renders below the Android status bar.

ch06_14/android/app/src/main/res/layout/fragment_map.xml

```
<?xml version="1.0" encoding="utf-8"?>
<androidx.constraintlayout.widget.ConstraintLayout
    xmlns:android="http://schemas.android.com/apk/res/android"
    xmlns:app="http://schemas.android.com/apk/res-auto"
    android:layout_width="match_parent"
    android:layout_height="match_parent"
    android:fitsSystemWindows="true">

    <com.google.android.material.appbar.AppBarLayout
        android:id="@+id/app_bar"
        android:layout_width="match_parent"
        android:layout_height="wrap_content"
        app:layout_constraintEnd_toEndOf="parent"
        app:layout_constraintStart_toStartOf="parent"
        app:layout_constraintTop_toTopOf="parent">

        <com.google.android.material.appbar.MaterialToolbar
            android:id="@+id/toolbar"
            android:layout_width="match_parent"
            android:layout_height="wrap_content" />
```

```
        </com.google.android.material.appbar.AppBarLayout>

        <androidx.compose.ui.platform.ComposeView
            android:id="@+id/compose_view"
            android:layout_width="match_parent"
            android:layout_height="0dp"
            app:layout_constraintBottom_toBottomOf="parent"
            app:layout_constraintTop_toBottomOf="@+id/app_bar" />

    </androidx.constraintlayout.widget.ConstraintLayout>
```

Ah, much better. Now let's replace that static text with an actual map.

Configure Google Maps with an API Key

Any integration with Google Maps, including Android apps, requires a few steps, specifically:

1. Create an API key with the Google Maps API enabled.
2. Create a secrets file to hold the API key securely.
3. Configure a plugin to read from this secret file.
4. Add the Google Maps dependencies.

Create your API key according to the instructions on the Google Developer site[3] or follow Emily Keller's helpful video.[4] Make sure to enable the Google Maps Platform APIs and SDKs for the API key, which will start with AIza.

We'll add the API key to the project with a secrets file. In Android Studio, expand Gradle Scripts and right-click local.properties. Select New → File and enter secrets.properties and press ↵, as shown in the screenshot on page 114.

Add your API key to this file like so:

```
MAPS_API_KEY=AIzaXXXXXX-XXXXXXXXXXXXXXXXXXXXXXXXXXXXX
```

---

3. https://developers.google.com/maps/documentation/android-sdk/get-api-key
4. https://youtu.be/2_HZObVbe-g

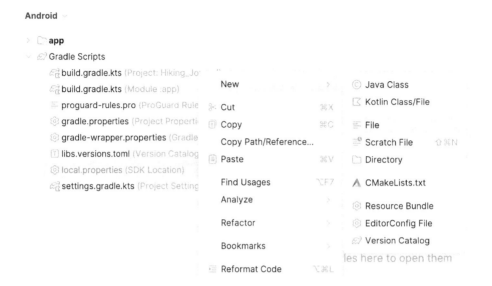

To keep the key secure, we won't check the secrets file into version control. Tell git to ignore it by appending secrets.properties to the bottom of .gitignore. Do this by running the following command from the android directory on the command line: echo secrets.properties >> .gitignore.

To reference the key, we'll use the Secrets Gradle plugin,[5] as recommended by Google. Add the plugin to the top of your app's build.gradle.kts and tell it where to find the secrets file.

```
ch06_15/android/app/build.gradle.kts
plugins {
    alias(libs.plugins.android.application)
    alias(libs.plugins.kotlin.android)
    alias(libs.plugins.compose.compiler)
    id("com.google.android.libraries.mapsplatform.secrets-gradle-plugin")
}

secrets {
    propertiesFileName = "secrets.properties"
}

// ...
```

While you're in this file, also add the Maps Compose Library[6] dependency at the bottom.

---

5. https://developers.google.com/maps/documentation/android-sdk/secrets-gradle-plugin
6. https://developers.google.com/maps/documentation/android-sdk/maps-compose

```
ch06_15/android/app/build.gradle.kts
// ...

dependencies {
    implementation(libs.androidx.core.ktx)
    implementation(libs.androidx.appcompat)
    implementation(libs.material)
    implementation(libs.androidx.activity)
    implementation(libs.androidx.constraintlayout)
    implementation("dev.hotwire:core:1.2.0")
    implementation("dev.hotwire:navigation-fragments:1.2.0")
    implementation(platform("androidx.compose:compose-bom:2025.04.01"))
    implementation("androidx.compose.material3:material3")
    implementation("androidx.compose.ui:ui-tooling-preview")
    implementation("com.google.maps.android:maps-compose:6.1.0")
    debugImplementation("androidx.compose.ui:ui-tooling")
    testImplementation(libs.junit)
    androidTestImplementation(libs.androidx.junit)
    androidTestImplementation(libs.androidx.espresso.core)
}
```

Then in the *project's* build.gradle.kts (the *first* one under Gradle Scripts), add the
secrets plugin as a build script dependency. Note that you don't have to split
the string into two lines like I did; I just find it easier to read.

```
ch06_15/android/build.gradle.kts
// Top-level build file where you can add configuration options common to all
// sub-projects/modules.
plugins {
    alias(libs.plugins.android.application) apply false
    alias(libs.plugins.kotlin.android) apply false
    alias(libs.plugins.compose.compiler) apply false
}
buildscript {
    dependencies {
        classpath(
            "com.google.android.libraries.mapsplatform" +
                    ".secrets-gradle-plugin:secrets-gradle-plugin:2.0.1"
        )
    }
}
```

Finally, open AndroidManifest.xml and set the Google Maps API key via MAPS_API_KEY
and sync Gradle.

```
ch06_15/android/app/src/main/AndroidManifest.xml
<?xml version="1.0" encoding="utf-8"?>
<manifest xmlns:android="http://schemas.android.com/apk/res/android"
    xmlns:tools="http://schemas.android.com/tools">

    <uses-permission android:name="android.permission.INTERNET" />
```

```
<application
    android:name=".HikingJournalApplication"
    android:allowBackup="true"
    android:dataExtractionRules="@xml/data_extraction_rules"
    android:fullBackupContent="@xml/backup_rules"
    android:icon="@mipmap/ic_launcher"
    android:label="@string/app_name"
    android:roundIcon="@mipmap/ic_launcher_round"
    android:supportsRtl="true"
    android:theme="@style/Theme.HikingJournal"
    android:usesCleartextTraffic="true"
    tools:targetApi="31">

    <activity
        android:name=".activities.MainActivity"
        android:exported="true">
        <intent-filter>
            <action android:name="android.intent.action.MAIN" />

            <category android:name="android.intent.category.LAUNCHER" />
        </intent-filter>
    </activity>

➤   <meta-data
➤       android:name="com.google.android.geo.API_KEY"
➤       android:value="${MAPS_API_KEY}" />
    </application>

</manifest>
```

Phew... Lots of configuration to configure Google Maps! Not a lot of fun, I know. Especially when we didn't have to do any of this on iOS. OK, enough complaining—back to the code. Let's get a map on the screen!

Add a Map to the View

Open MapFragment.kt and replace Text() with GoogleMap(). Sadly, Google Maps doesn't work in the Compose Preview, so go ahead and remove the @Preview decoration on the function, too.

ch06_16/android/app/src/main/java/com/masilotti/hikingjournal/fragments/MapFragment.kt
```
// ...
import androidx.compose.ui.platform.ComposeView
➤ import com.google.maps.android.compose.GoogleMap
import com.masilotti.hikingjournal.R
import dev.hotwire.navigation.destinations.HotwireDestinationDeepLink
import dev.hotwire.navigation.fragments.HotwireFragment

@HotwireDestinationDeepLink(uri = "hotwire://fragment/map")
class MapFragment : HotwireFragment() {
    // ...
}
```

```
@Composable
fun MapView() {
➤    GoogleMap()
}
```

We'll position the map with a coordinate, just as we did with the SwiftUI view.
Wrap a LatLng in a call to rememberCameraPositionState() to ensure the map doesn't
reset when switching between apps.

ch06_17/android/app/src/main/java/com/masilotti/hikingjournal/fragments/MapFragment.kt
```
// ...
import androidx.compose.ui.platform.ComposeView
➤ import com.google.android.gms.maps.model.CameraPosition
➤ import com.google.android.gms.maps.model.LatLng
import com.google.maps.android.compose.GoogleMap
➤ import com.google.maps.android.compose.rememberCameraPositionState
import com.masilotti.hikingjournal.R
import dev.hotwire.navigation.destinations.HotwireDestinationDeepLink
import dev.hotwire.navigation.fragments.HotwireFragment

@HotwireDestinationDeepLink(uri = "hotwire://fragment/map")
class MapFragment : HotwireFragment() {
    // ...
}

@Composable
fun MapView() {
➤    val coordinate = LatLng(45.511881, -122.595706)
➤    val cameraPositionState = rememberCameraPositionState {
➤        position = CameraPosition.fromLatLngZoom(coordinate, 15f)
➤    }
➤    GoogleMap(cameraPositionState = cameraPositionState)
}
```

Next, add a map marker at the same position.

ch06_18/android/app/src/main/java/com/masilotti/hikingjournal/fragments/MapFragment.kt
```
// ...
import com.google.maps.android.compose.GoogleMap
➤ import com.google.maps.android.compose.Marker
import com.google.maps.android.compose.rememberCameraPositionState
➤ import com.google.maps.android.compose.rememberMarkerState
import com.masilotti.hikingjournal.R
import dev.hotwire.navigation.destinations.HotwireDestinationDeepLink
import dev.hotwire.navigation.fragments.HotwireFragment

@HotwireDestinationDeepLink(uri = "hotwire://fragment/map")
class MapFragment : HotwireFragment() {
    // ...
}

@Composable
fun MapView() {
```

```
        val coordinate = LatLng(45.511881, -122.595706)
        val markerState = rememberMarkerState(position = coordinate)
        val cameraPositionState = rememberCameraPositionState {
            position = CameraPosition.fromLatLngZoom(coordinate, 15f)
        }
        GoogleMap(cameraPositionState = cameraPositionState) {
            Marker(
                state = markerState,
                title = "Mount Tabor"
            )
        }
    }
}
```

Finally, replicate our design on iOS by using a hybrid map type.

ch06_19/android/app/src/main/java/com/masilotti/hikingjournal/fragments/MapFragment.kt
```
// ...
import com.google.maps.android.compose.GoogleMap
import com.google.maps.android.compose.MapProperties
import com.google.maps.android.compose.MapType
import com.google.maps.android.compose.Marker
// ...

@HotwireDestinationDeepLink(uri = "hotwire://fragment/map")
class MapFragment : HotwireFragment() {
    // ...
}

@Composable
fun MapView() {
    val coordinate = LatLng(45.511881, -122.595706)
    val markerState = rememberMarkerState(position = coordinate)
    val cameraPositionState = rememberCameraPositionState {
        position = CameraPosition.fromLatLngZoom(coordinate, 15f)
    }
    GoogleMap(
        cameraPositionState = cameraPositionState,
        properties = MapProperties(mapType = MapType.HYBRID)
    ) {
        Marker(
            state = markerState,
            title = "Mount Tabor"
        )
    }
}
```

Alright, see the screenshot on page 119, you've got yourself a map! Now, let's make it useful by making it dynamic based on the hike.

Fetch and Parse JSON with Model and View Model

As expected, we'll model our approach on what we did for iOS. Start by creating a new Kotlin Data class under the models package named Hike.kt. Add an attribute for name, latitude, and longitude.

ch06_20/android/app/src/main/java/com/masilotti/hikingjournal/models/Hike.kt
```
package com.masilotti.hikingjournal.models

data class Hike(
    val name: String,
    val latitude: Double,
    val longitude: Double
)
```

Then, expose the coordinate via a computed property. We'll use this to initialize the LatLng when positioning the map.

ch06_21/android/app/src/main/java/com/masilotti/hikingjournal/models/Hike.kt
```
package com.masilotti.hikingjournal.models

import com.google.android.gms.maps.model.LatLng

data class Hike(
```

```
    val name: String,
    val latitude: Double,
    val longitude: Double
) {
    val coordinate: LatLng
        get() = LatLng(latitude, longitude)
}
```

Continuing our mental model from iOS, we'll use a view model to fetch data from our server and populate the model.

If you skipped Chapter 5, Render Native Screens with SwiftUI, on page 81, then make sure you add the following to your Rails app at app/views/maps/show.json.jbuilder. This provides the JSON needed for each hike's map.

ch05_10/rails/app/views/maps/show.json.jbuilder
```
json.extract! @hike, :name, :latitude, :longitude
```

Create a new package named viewmodels and add a Kotlin file named HikeView-Model.kt that implements ViewModel. Initialize this with a URL String—this will point to the JSON endpoint that exposes the hike's attributes.

ch06_22/android/app/src/main/java/com/masilotti/hikingjournal/viewmodels/HikeViewModel.kt
```
package com.masilotti.hikingjournal.viewmodels

import androidx.lifecycle.ViewModel

class HikeViewModel(private val url: String) : ViewModel() {
}
```

Next, add a property to the view model that references an instance of Hike. Using mutableStateOf() ensures that when this property is updated, the changes will propagate to the view, just like the @Observable keyword we used in Swift.

ch06_23/android/app/src/main/java/com/masilotti/hikingjournal/viewmodels/HikeViewModel.kt
```
package com.masilotti.hikingjournal.viewmodels

import androidx.compose.runtime.mutableStateOf
import androidx.lifecycle.ViewModel
import com.masilotti.hikingjournal.models.Hike

class HikeViewModel(private val url: String) : ViewModel() {
    var hike = mutableStateOf<Hike?>(null)
        private set
}
```

To initiate the network request, add an empty function named fetchCoordinates(). Fetching data from the server will happen asynchronously, so add the suspend keyword to "wait" for this execution to finish when called.

ch06_24/android/app/src/main/java/com/masilotti/hikingjournal/viewmodels/HikeViewModel.kt

```
package com.masilotti.hikingjournal.viewmodels

import androidx.compose.runtime.mutableStateOf
import androidx.lifecycle.ViewModel
import com.masilotti.hikingjournal.models.Hike

class HikeViewModel(private val url: String) : ViewModel() {
    var hike = mutableStateOf<Hike?>(null)
        private set

➤    suspend fun fetchCoordinates() {
➤    }
}
```

Implement the function by reading text from the initialized url. Parse the response to create a new Hike instance and assign it to the hike property's value.

ch06_25/android/app/src/main/java/com/masilotti/hikingjournal/viewmodels/HikeViewModel.kt

```
package com.masilotti.hikingjournal.viewmodels

import androidx.compose.runtime.mutableStateOf
import androidx.lifecycle.ViewModel
import com.masilotti.hikingjournal.models.Hike
➤ import kotlinx.coroutines.Dispatchers
➤ import kotlinx.coroutines.withContext
➤ import org.json.JSONObject
➤ import java.net.URL

class HikeViewModel(private val url: String) : ViewModel() {
    var hike = mutableStateOf<Hike?>(null)
        private set

    suspend fun fetchCoordinates() {
➤        val data = withContext(Dispatchers.IO) {
➤            URL(url).readText()
➤        }
➤        val json = JSONObject(data)
➤        hike.value = Hike(
➤            name = json.getString("name"),
➤            latitude = json.getDouble("latitude"),
➤            longitude = json.getDouble("longitude")
➤        )
    }
}
```

Just to be safe, add some rudimentary error handling that prints the stack trace of any exceptions that occur.

ch06_26/android/app/src/main/java/com/masilotti/hikingjournal/viewmodels/HikeViewModel.kt

```
class HikeViewModel(private val url: String) : ViewModel() {
    var hike = mutableStateOf<Hike?>(null)
        private set
```

```
    suspend fun fetchCoordinates() {
        try {
            val data = withContext(Dispatchers.IO) {
                URL(url).readText()
            }
            val json = JSONObject(data)
            hike.value = Hike(
                name = json.getString("name"),
                latitude = json.getDouble("latitude"),
                longitude = json.getDouble("longitude")
            )
        } catch (e: Exception) {
            e.printStackTrace()
        }
    }
}
```

OK, view model done. Connect it to the fragment by adding a mutable property to MapFragment.kt.

ch06_27/android/app/src/main/java/com/masilotti/hikingjournal/fragments/MapFragment.kt

```
// ...
import com.google.maps.android.compose.rememberMarkerState
import com.masilotti.hikingjournal.R
import com.masilotti.hikingjournal.viewmodels.HikeViewModel
import dev.hotwire.navigation.destinations.HotwireDestinationDeepLink
import dev.hotwire.navigation.fragments.HotwireFragment

@HotwireDestinationDeepLink(uri = "hotwire://fragment/map")
class MapFragment : HotwireFragment() {
    private lateinit var viewModel: HikeViewModel

    override fun onCreateView(
        inflater: LayoutInflater,
        container: ViewGroup?,
        savedInstanceState: Bundle?
    ): View {
        viewModel = HikeViewModel(url = "${navigator.location}.json")

        val view = inflater.inflate(R.layout.fragment_map, container, false)
        view.findViewById<ComposeView>(R.id.compose_view).apply {
            setContent {
                MapView()
            }
        }
        return view
    }
}
// ...
```

This fragment subclasses HotwireFragment, which grants us access to a Navigator instance. Navigator.location provides the most recently visited URL string, which we append the JSON extension to and pass to the view model. lateinit defers initialization of the view model until we have the URL string ready.

The @Composable function at the bottom of the file exists on its own—it's not a part of MapFragment. For it to use the view model, we need to pass a reference along when invoked.

ch06_28/android/app/src/main/java/com/masilotti/hikingjournal/fragments/MapFragment.kt

```
// ...

@HotwireDestinationDeepLink(uri = "hotwire://fragment/map")
class MapFragment : HotwireFragment() {
    private lateinit var viewModel: HikeViewModel

    override fun onCreateView(
        inflater: LayoutInflater,
        container: ViewGroup?,
        savedInstanceState: Bundle?
    ): View {
        viewModel = HikeViewModel(url = "${navigator.location}.json")

        val view = inflater.inflate(R.layout.fragment_map, container, false)
        view.findViewById<ComposeView>(R.id.compose_view).apply {
            setContent {
                MapView(viewModel = viewModel)
            }
        }
        return view
    }
}

@Composable
fun MapView(viewModel: HikeViewModel) {
    // ...
}
```

Now, we can change the hardcoded marker, camera, and title values to the ones retrieved from the view model.

ch06_29/android/app/src/main/java/com/masilotti/hikingjournal/fragments/MapFragment.kt

```
// ...
@HotwireDestinationDeepLink(uri = "hotwire://fragment/map")
class MapFragment : HotwireFragment() {
    // ...
}

@Composable
fun MapView(viewModel: HikeViewModel) {
    val hike = viewModel.hike.value
    if (hike != null) {
```

```
        val markerState = rememberMarkerState(position = hike.coordinate)
        val cameraPositionState = rememberCameraPositionState {
            position = CameraPosition.fromLatLngZoom(hike.coordinate, 15f)
        }
        GoogleMap(
            cameraPositionState = cameraPositionState,
            properties = MapProperties(mapType = MapType.HYBRID)
        ) {
            Marker(
                state = markerState,
                title = hike.name
            )
        }
    }
}
```

Before you run the app, do you know what will happen? I'll give you a hint: We ran into the exact same problem on iOS. That's right—we never told our view model to fetch the data from the server!

Call fetchCoordinates() on the view model, and then wrap it in a LaunchedEffect. This ensures any changes to the underlying mutableStateOf<Hike?>() bubble up to the fragment and re-render the @Composable.

ch06_30/android/app/src/main/java/com/masilotti/hikingjournal/fragments/MapFragment.kt
```
// ...
import androidx.compose.runtime.Composable
import androidx.compose.runtime.LaunchedEffect
import androidx.compose.ui.platform.ComposeView
// ...

@HotwireDestinationDeepLink(uri = "hotwire://fragment/map")
class MapFragment : HotwireFragment() {
    // ...
}

@Composable
fun MapView(viewModel: HikeViewModel) {
    LaunchedEffect(viewModel) {
        viewModel.fetchCoordinates()
    }

    val hike = viewModel.hike.value
    if (hike != null) {
        // ...
    }
}
```

And now you have a dynamic map on Android, as shown in the screenshot on page 125. Great work—that was a *lot* of mucking around in Android Studio!

Integrating Jetpack Compose with Hotwire Native requires a fair amount of code and a lot of configuration. The good news is that next time you can skip all the setup and jump right into the Kotlin code. You'll create a new Fragment that holds your ComposeView and @Composable. Then, you will register the fragment with Hotwire Native and add @HotwireDestinationDeepLink to match the uri in your path configuration. To get data, a view model will fetch JSON from your server and populate a model via mutableStateOf() and LaunchedEffect.

What's Next?

As I mentioned at the end of Chapter 5, Render Native Screens with SwiftUI, on page 81, you can use this approach to build any native screen or interaction you want. You could swap out the map and render data from the Health Platform API. Or convert the list of hikes to native elements and cache it for offline access. The list goes on.

But because of how expensive native screens are to build, each native feature should only be reserved for the most critical pieces of your app.

The good news is that there is a middle ground. When you want a little extra fidelity, you can upgrade individual *components* to native without committing to an entire SwiftUI or Jetpack Compose screen. The next chapter covers how to integrate bridge components to add native buttons to your app.

A heads up that even if you're only working through the Android side of things, you'll still need to read through Chapter 7, Build iOS Bridge Components with Swift, on page 127. It introduces concepts and code that are required for building bridge components with Android.

Build iOS Bridge Components with Swift

You just learned how to build fully native screens with SwiftUI and Jetpack Compose. And as I'm sure you noticed, there's a *lot* of code needed to get it all working. Not to mention coordinating deploys between your Rails APIs and the apps in the app stores.

So what's a savvy hybrid app developer like yourself to do if you only need a native component or two? Say you want to level up your sign-in screen with a native button in the navigation bar at the top. Enter bridge components. They unlock *progressive enhancement* of individual controls without converting entire screens to native. Bridge components strike a nice balance between HTML screens and fully native ones. They require less upfront code to get working and, when built correctly, can be sprinkled onto new screens without needing native code updates. This means less code to write and less code to maintain.

Here are two examples from the hotwire-native-ios demo app.[1] For each, the web-based HTML is on the left and the bridge component is on the right.

The first example is a simple form, as shown in the first set of screenshots on page 128.

On the left, the web-based submit button is at the bottom. On the right, it's replaced with a native component in the upper right. This not only makes the app feel more native but ensures the keyboard doesn't hide the button when editing a form field, as shown in the second set of screenshots on page 128.

---

1. https://github.com/hotwired/hotwire-native-ios/tree/main/Demo

In our second example, an HTML-based dialog (on the left) is converted to a native action sheet (on the right), which feels much more at home in an iOS app. Using the native control also darkens the entire screen a bit (including the native navigation bar at the top), giving an even cleaner look than the web-based approach.

Source Code for Bridge Components

 The full source code for each of these components can be found in the Hotwire Native iOS[2] and Android[3] repositories under the Demo app directory.

So, what actually *is* a bridge component?

Bridge components are comprised of two complementary sides: the web side and the client side. On the web, you'll work with a special subclass of a Stimulus controller[4] configured with a bit of HTML. And on the client, you'll write Swift (or Kotlin if building an Android app) to interact with native APIs.

Breaking this down, each bridge component requires three building blocks:

1. The HTML markup—where your server configures the component.

---

2. https://github.com/hotwired/hotwire-native-ios/tree/main/Demo
3. https://github.com/hotwired/hotwire-native-android/tree/main/demo
4. https://stimulus.hotwired.dev

2. The Stimulus controller subclass—where messages are passed between web and native.

3. The native component—where Swift/Kotlin generates the UI and interacts with native APIs.

Stimulus.js

 If you aren't comfortable working with Stimulus, then now is a good time to brush up on the basics. I recommend reading through the official handbook[5] before moving on.

This chapter walks through building a native button component to submit forms and navigate to new pages. Here is an example of what the sign-in screen will look like before (left) and after (right) working through this chapter:

In this chapter, you'll build the iOS bridge component with Swift. But before you can do that, you need to configure the server.

Install Hotwire Native Bridge

We need one JavaScript package on the web to get started. Install the Hotwire Native Bridge for web[6] library from the rails directory by running the following command:

```
bin/importmap pin @hotwired/hotwire-native-bridge
```

If you aren't using import maps in your Rails application, then review the installation instructions[7] for more details on how to work with the dependency.

With your server configured, you can build a new bridge component by following these steps:

1. Add the HTML markup.

---

5. https://stimulus.hotwired.dev/handbook/introduction
6. https://github.com/hotwired/hotwire-native-bridge
7. https://native.hotwired.dev/reference/bridge-installation

2. Create a Stimulus controller.

3. Create a native component.

Add the HTML Markup

Start by adding the HTML markup to the sign-in form. Open app/views/sessions/new.html.erb in the Rails app and add the controller data attribute to the submit button.

```
ch07_02/rails/app/views/sessions/new.html.erb
<% content_for :title, "Sign in" %>

<div class="container d-flex flex-column mw-400 mx-auto">
  <h1 class="h3 d-hotwire-native-none my-4 mx-auto">
    Sign in to your account
  </h1>

  <%= form_with url: session_path, class: "row g-3 mt-1" do |form| %>
    <%# ... %>

    <div>
➤     <%= form.submit "Sign in", class: "btn btn-primary w-100", data: {
➤       controller: "bridge--button"
➤     } %>
    </div>
  <% end %>
</div>
```

Data Attributes in Rails

In Rails we can write data attributes a few different ways. The following two code snippets both generate the same HTML:

```
<a href="#" data-controller="button" data-foo-bar="baz">Click</a>
```

The standard approach is to use a separate data-* for each attribute:

```
<%= link_to "Click", "#",
  "data-controller": "button",
  "data-foo-bar": "baz" %>
```

And a second approach is to use a single data key pointing to a hash. This way also converts underscores in the keys to dashes, allowing us to use Ruby symbols as keys (instead of "foo-bar").

```
<%= link_to "Click", "#", data: {
  controller: "button",
  foo_bar: "baz"
} %>
```

I prefer the second approach because we can group all of our data attributes in a single hash. I also think it looks a bit cleaner.

Note the double dashes (--) when referencing the Stimulus controller. This allows us to namespace our bridge component controllers under the bridge/ directory, keeping them separate from traditional Stimulus controllers.

Create a Stimulus Controller

Next, create a new Stimulus controller by running the following command from the rails directory:

```
bin/rails generate stimulus bridge/button
```

This creates a new file at app/javascript/controllers/bridge/button_controller.js. Remember, the nested bridge directory helps us separate web-only Stimulus controllers from bridge components.

Open the controller and replace the import statements with those from the newly added JavaScript library. Also, change the base class to BridgeComponent.

ch07_03/rails/app/javascript/controllers/bridge/button_controller.js
```
➤ import { BridgeComponent } from "@hotwired/hotwire-native-bridge"

➤ export default class extends BridgeComponent {
}
```

Next, set the component's identifier to "button". You'll do the same in the native component, the common name wiring the two pieces together.

ch07_04/rails/app/javascript/controllers/bridge/button_controller.js
```
import { BridgeComponent } from "@hotwired/hotwire-native-bridge"

export default class extends BridgeComponent {
➤   static component = "button"
}
```

As with most Stimulus controllers, we'll do our configuration in connect(). Add this function and don't forget to call super—BridgeComponent is an extension of a Stimulus controller, after all.

ch07_05/rails/app/javascript/controllers/bridge/button_controller.js
```
import { BridgeComponent } from "@hotwired/hotwire-native-bridge"

export default class extends BridgeComponent {
  static component = "button"

➤   connect() {
➤     super.connect()
➤   }
}
```

To communicate with the native component, we'll use the send() function from BridgeComponent, which takes three parameters:

1. The name of the message to send
2. An options *object* (or "hash", in Ruby terms)
3. An optional callback function

At the end of connect(), call send() with "connect" as the first parameter, followed by an empty options object and an empty callback function.

ch07_06/rails/app/javascript/controllers/bridge/button_controller.js
```javascript
import { BridgeComponent } from "@hotwired/hotwire-native-bridge"

export default class extends BridgeComponent {
  static component = "button"

  connect() {
    super.connect()

    this.send("connect", {}, () => {
    })
  }
}
```

We'll come back and add more to this later in the chapter. But for now, let's create the third building block—the native counterpart—to make sure everything is wired up correctly between the web side and the client side.

Create a Native Component

In the iOS app, create a new directory under App and name it Components. Inside, create a new Swift file named ButtonComponent.swift. Replace the contents with the following:

ch07_07/ios/App/Components/ButtonComponent.swift
```swift
import HotwireNative
import UIKit

class ButtonComponent: BridgeComponent {
}
```

Next, identify this component as "button", just like on the web.

ch07_08/ios/App/Components/ButtonComponent.swift
```swift
import HotwireNative
import UIKit

class ButtonComponent: BridgeComponent {
    override class var name: String { "button" }
}
```

Unlike the web, we have to manually register this component with Hotwire Native. Open AppDelegate.swift and register this bridge component after setting up the path configuration.

ch07_09/ios/App/Delegates/AppDelegate.swift
```
import HotwireNative
import UIKit

@main
class AppDelegate: UIResponder, UIApplicationDelegate {
    func application(
        _ application: UIApplication,
        didFinishLaunchingWithOptions launchOptions:
        [UIApplication.LaunchOptionsKey: Any]?
    ) -> Bool {
        Hotwire.loadPathConfiguration(from: [
            .server(baseURL.appending(path: "configurations/ios_v1.json"))
        ])

        Hotwire.registerBridgeComponents([
            ButtonComponent.self
        ])

        return true
    }
}
```

Under the hood, this appends bridge-components: ["button"] to the user agent of requests coming from the app. The Hotwire Native Bridge uses this string to identify which components an app supports. connect() won't be called for a component that isn't registered in the user agent, like on mobile web. But more on that later.

Back in ButtonComponent.swift, add an empty function to start receiving messages. Every time send() is called from the Stimulus controller on the web, onReceive(message:) gets called on iOS.

ch07_10/ios/App/Components/ButtonComponent.swift
```
import HotwireNative
import UIKit

class ButtonComponent: BridgeComponent {
    override class var name: String { "button" }

    override func onReceive(message: Message) {
    }
}
```

A quick way to validate that this is working is to add a static button to the screen. Inside of onReceive(message:), add a native navigation bar button item. We'll make this button text dynamic later in the chapter.

ch07_11/ios/App/Components/ButtonComponent.swift

```swift
import HotwireNative
import UIKit

class ButtonComponent: BridgeComponent {
    override class var name: String { "button" }

    override func onReceive(message: Message) {
        let button = UIBarButtonItem(title: "Sign in")

        let viewController = delegate?.destination as? UIViewController
        viewController?.navigationItem.rightBarButtonItem = button
    }
}
```

To add native elements to the screen, we needed a reference to a UIViewController. delegate.destination provided us with just the hook we needed—all we had to do was cast it to a controller.

Run the app and click the Sign in button at the bottom of the screen. On the sign-in screen, the new native component will appear in the upper right.

Too bad it doesn't do anything! We'll fix that next.

But before we move on, this is a good checkpoint to stop and reflect. You now have the three building blocks of a bridge component: the HTML markup, the Stimulus controller on the web, and the native component in the iOS app. The rest of the chapter will focus on *customizing* the component to do something more than adding a (useless!) button to the screen.

Customize the Component

Up next, we'll walk through how to customize the bridge component in the following ways:

• Respond to button taps.

- Make the button text dynamic.
- Hide the HTML version of the button.
- Add a dynamic image.
- Fix some bugs along the way.

Respond to Button Taps

On the web, we used send() to pass a message *to* native code. To pass a message *from* native code to the web, we have reply(to:). Call this via a UIAction, which fires when the button is tapped.

ch07_12/ios/App/Components/ButtonComponent.swift
```swift
import HotwireNative
import UIKit

class ButtonComponent: BridgeComponent {
    override class var name: String { "button" }

    override func onReceive(message: Message) {
        let action = UIAction(title: "Sign in") { _ in
            self.reply(to: message.event)
        }
        let button = UIBarButtonItem(primaryAction: action)

        let viewController = delegate?.destination as? UIViewController
        viewController?.navigationItem.rightBarButtonItem = button
    }
}
```

Note that we also moved the title, "Sign in", from the button to the action. If we had set both, then the title of the UIAction would take precedence over the button's title. So, to not duplicate code, we're only setting the title on the action.

Back in the Rails codebase, open button_controller.js. In the body of the callback function, *click* the bridge element, like so:

ch07_12/rails/app/javascript/controllers/bridge/button_controller.js
```javascript
import { BridgeComponent } from "@hotwired/hotwire-native-bridge"

export default class extends BridgeComponent {
  static component = "button"

  connect() {
    super.connect()

    this.send("connect", {}, () => {
      this.bridgeElement.click()
    })
  }
}
```

this.bridgeElement wraps the attached HTML element, the one we added the controller data attribute to, in a BridgeElement instance. Using this, we can grab the title, check if it's disabled, and even click it. Check out the documentation on Bridge Elements[8] and Data Attributes[9] for more info on what bridge elements can do.

Hop back into Xcode and run the app. Open the sign-in screen and tap "Sign in" at the top right. The sign-in form will submit as if you tapped the HTML submit button. Nice work—your first functional bridge component!

Right now, the native Sign in button pretty much only works as, well, a Sign in button since we hardcoded the title in Swift. This kind of defeats the purpose of bridge components: they're supposed to be dynamic components driven by HTML. Let's change that by setting the title of the button from the server.

Make the Button Text Dynamic

First, add a line of markup to the HTML file we were working on earlier, app/views/sessions/new.html.erb, setting the data-bridge-title attribute. Remember, Rails will convert the underscores in this hash to dashes.

ch07_13/rails/app/views/sessions/new.html.erb
```erb
<% content_for :title, "Sign in" %>

<div class="container d-flex flex-column mw-400 mx-auto">
  <h1 class="h3 d-hotwire-native-none my-4 mx-auto">
    Sign in to your account
  </h1>

  <%= form_with url: session_path, class: "row g-3 mt-1" do |form| %>
    <%# ... %>

    <div>
      <%= form.submit "Sign in", class: "btn btn-primary w-100", data: {
        controller: "bridge--button",
        bridge_title: "Sign in"
      } %>
    </div>
  <% end %>
</div>
```

Remember the BridgeElement that we *clicked* before? We can call bridgeElement.title to grab the value of data-bridge-title set in the HTML.

---

8. https://native.hotwired.dev/reference/bridge-components#bridge-elements
9. https://native.hotwired.dev/reference/bridge-components#data-attributes

Open button_controller.js and pass the title in the second parameter of send(). I'm using JavaScript's shorthand property names to create this object: {title: title}.

ch07_13/rails/app/javascript/controllers/bridge/button_controller.js
```
import { BridgeComponent } from "@hotwired/hotwire-native-bridge"

export default class extends BridgeComponent {
  static component = "button"

  connect() {
    super.connect()

    const title = this.bridgeElement.bridgeAttribute("title")
    this.send("connect", {title}, () => {
      this.bridgeElement.click()
    })
  }
}
```

Now that our title is coming over the wire, next up is to pass it to the UIAction. Open ButtonComponent.swift in Xcode and add a new struct to the bottom of the file:

ch07_14/ios/App/Components/ButtonComponent.swift
```
import HotwireNative
import UIKit

class ButtonComponent: BridgeComponent {
    override class var name: String { "button" }

    override func onReceive(message: Message) {
        let action = UIAction(title: "Sign in") { _ in
            self.reply(to: message.event)
        }
        let button = UIBarButtonItem(primaryAction: action)

        let viewController = delegate?.destination as? UIViewController
        viewController?.navigationItem.rightBarButtonItem = button
    }
}

private extension ButtonComponent {
    struct MessageData: Decodable {
        let title: String
    }
}
```

This MessageData struct is nested under an extension to ButtonComponent. This is Swift's way of namespacing entities: it translates to ButtonComponent.MessageData.

The struct itself implements the Decodable protocol, enabling JSON deserialization. This is perfect because the JavaScript sent from our Stimulus controller comes in as JSON. Inside the struct, there's a single String property: the title of the button.

Inside of onReceive(message:), create an instance of MessageData by calling data() on Message. Then, pass that along to the UIAction to set the title of the button:

```
ch07_15/ios/App/Components/ButtonComponent.swift
import HotwireNative
import UIKit

class ButtonComponent: BridgeComponent {
    override class var name: String { "button" }

    override func onReceive(message: Message) {
        guard let data: MessageData = message.data() else { return }

        let action = UIAction(title: data.title) { _ in
            self.reply(to: message.event)
        }
        let button = UIBarButtonItem(primaryAction: action)

        let viewController = delegate?.destination as? UIViewController
        viewController?.navigationItem.rightBarButtonItem = button
    }
}

private extension ButtonComponent {
    struct MessageData: Decodable {
        let title: String
    }
}
```

The guard statement ensures that, if the JSON deserialization fails, the function will return early and not add a native button.

Run the app again and visit the Sign in page. The native button title will still read "Sign in," but this time it's coming from the HTML instead of being hardcoded in Swift.

Prove this by changing the value of data-bridge-title in app/views/sessions/new.html.erb. Dismiss the modal and visit the Sign in page again—the new button title will appear, all without even rerunning the native app.

Looking good! Well, except for the fact that there are now *two* buttons to sign in: a native one in the upper right and the big blue HTML one at the bottom.

Hide the HTML Button

We can hide the HTML button with some custom, albeit complicated-looking, CSS. Add the following to the end of the native CSS file, app/assets/stylesheets/native.css:

```
ch07_16/rails/app/assets/stylesheets/native.css
.d-hotwire-native-none {
  display: none !important;
}

.d-hotwire-native-block {
  display: block !important;
}
[data-bridge-components~="button"]
[data-controller~="bridge--button"] {
  display: none !important;
}
```

If you're wondering what in the world is going on here, well, you're not alone. Let's break it down line by line.

Remember when registering our bridge components added bridge-components: ["button"] to the user agent? The Hotwire Native Bridge uses this to add custom data attributes to the <html> element via JavaScript.

```
<html data-bridge-platform="ios" data-bridge-components="button">
```

The first line of new CSS, [data-bridge-components~="button"], uses these data attributes on <html> to make sure the web view is equipped to handle a "button" component. The second line, [data-controller~="bridge--button"], finds elements with data-controller set to "button". Together, these lines target the button element only for clients capable of handling this bridge component.

This means if the client does *not* register a "button" component, then the HTML button will remain visible. It only hides elements where a native button takes its place. This gives us a nice safety net when progressively upgrading components to native—older clients won't lose functionality; they will continue to use the pre-upgraded web interactions.

Now, before we go and make this component even better, let's take a second to reflect on how powerful this technique is. We can now add a *native* button to any page of our app *with only HTML.* Slap a data-controller="bridge--button" on something and boom—native button. And because the native interaction *actually clicks the web element*, we get all the behavior associated with it for free. Here, we're submitting a form, but we could execute some JavaScript, link to a new page, or anything else we can do on the web!

Practice this by making the "Add a hike" button a native one. Add the data markup to app/views/hikes/index.html.erb:

```
ch07_17/rails/app/views/hikes/index.html.erb
<%= render "shared/header", title: "Hikes" %>
<%# ... %>

<div class="container d-flex justify-content-between gap-2 mt-4">
  <% if user_signed_in? %>
    <%= link_to "Add a hike", new_hike_path,
      class: "btn btn-primary flex-grow-1 flex-sm-grow-0", data: {
        controller: "bridge--button",
        bridge_title: "Add"
      } %>
    <%# ... %>
  <% else %>
    <%# ... %>
  <% end %>
</div>
```

Run the app, sign in, and notice the native Add button in the upper right.

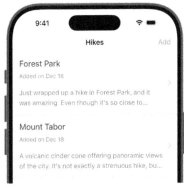

You just added a new, native button without a single line of native code. Ah, the magic of bridge components.

Text buttons work pretty well. But sometimes a simple, easily recognizable icon can level up the design. Next, we'll add an *image* to the bridge component powered by SF Symbols, the image set we used for the tab icons in Chapter 4, Add a Native Tab Bar, on page 61.

Add a Dynamic Image

Start by adding the bridge-image-name data attribute to the "Add a hike" button in the hike index view, app/views/hikes/index.html.erb. Here, we're indicating the name "plus". This will map to the corresponding SF Symbol name that we want to display in the app:

ch07_18/rails/app/views/hikes/index.html.erb
```
<%= render "shared/header", title: "Hikes" %>
<%# ... %>

<div class="container d-flex justify-content-between gap-2 mt-4">
  <% if user_signed_in? %>
    <%= link_to "Add a hike", new_hike_path,
      class: "btn btn-primary flex-grow-1 flex-sm-grow-0", data: {
        controller: "bridge--button",
        bridge_title: "Add",
        bridge_image_name: "plus"
      } %>
    <%# ... %>
  <% else %>
    <%# ... %>
  <% end %>
</div>
```

In button_controller.js, extract image-name from the BridgeElement and pass it to the call to send(), like so:

ch07_18/rails/app/javascript/controllers/bridge/button_controller.js
```
import { BridgeComponent } from "@hotwired/hotwire-native-bridge"

export default class extends BridgeComponent {
  static component = "button"

  connect() {
    super.connect()

    const title = this.bridgeElement.bridgeAttribute("title")
    const imageName = this.bridgeElement.bridgeAttribute("image-name")
    this.send("connect", {title, imageName}, () => {
      this.bridgeElement.click()
    })
  }
}
```

We're now sending a second JSON field, imageName, to the iOS app. To use this, we'll need to add a property in the Swift struct at the bottom of the file. Then we can pass it to the UIAction to set the image.

```
ch07_18/ios/App/Components/ButtonComponent.swift
import HotwireNative
import UIKit

class ButtonComponent: BridgeComponent {
    override class var name: String { "button" }

    override func onReceive(message: Message) {
        guard let data: MessageData = message.data() else { return }

        let action = UIAction(title: data.title) { _ in
            self.reply(to: message.event)
        }
        let button = UIBarButtonItem(primaryAction: action)

        if let imageName = data.imageName {
            button.image = UIImage(systemName: imageName)
        }

        let viewController = delegate?.destination as? UIViewController
        viewController?.navigationItem.rightBarButtonItem = button
    }
}

private extension ButtonComponent {
    struct MessageData: Decodable {
        let title: String
        let imageName: String?
    }
}
```

We're using an optional value, hence the question mark after String, because not all buttons will have an image—some will only use the title text.

Give the app a run, and you'll see a plus sign in the upper right. When tapped, this icon will add a new hike like before.

Go ahead and apply the same technique to the submit button on the hike form, app/views/hikes/_form.html.erb. Here, we're only using a title, so the "Save" text will appear on the native button.

ch07_19/rails/app/views/hikes/_form.html.erb
```
<%= form_with model: hike, class: "row g-3 mt-1" do |form| %>
  <%# ... %>

  <div class="d-grid d-sm-flex justify-content-sm-end mt-4">
    <%= form.submit "Save", class: "btn btn-primary", data: {
      controller: "bridge--button",
      bridge_title: "Save"
    } %>
  </div>
<% end %>
```

Continue by doing the same for the hike show page, app/views/hikes/show.html.erb. Here, we'll use a pencil icon to convey editing the hike.

ch07_19/rails/app/views/hikes/show.html.erb
```
<%= render "shared/header", title: @hike.name %>

<div class="container">
  <%# ... %>

  <div class="d-flex align-items-center mt-3">
    <%= render "likes/like", hike: @hike, like: @like %>

    <div class="d-flex gap-2 ms-auto">
      <%# ... %>

      <% if user_signed_in? && @hike.user == current_user %>
        <%= link_to edit_hike_path(@hike), class: "btn btn-outline-primary",
          data: {
            controller: "bridge--button",
            bridge_title: "Edit",
            bridge_image_name: "pencil"
          } do %>
          <i class="bi bi-pencil"></i>
          Edit
        <% end %>
      <% end %>
    </div>
  </div>

  <p class="text-body-secondary mt-4">
    <%= @hike.description %>
  </p>
</div>
```

These changes are shown in the screenshot on page 145.

Adding the edit icon (the pencil) to the hikes show page is a great example of how powerful bridge components are. This component should only appear when the user is signed in. And we can keep *all* of that logic on the server. Right now, it's embedded in the if user_signed_in? call in the app/views/hikes/index.html.erb template.

The native app code doesn't care if the user is signed in or not. If it receives the connect() message, it adds the component; that's all it needs to know. It doesn't need to perform any authentication checks or keep track of the authentication state; it simply waits for a message.

But there's a subtle bug. Can you find it?

Run the app, sign in, then sign back out. The native component is still there. And tapping it doesn't do anything.

Remove the Component on Disconnect

The component exists in the native part of the screen, the navigation bar. But when we sign out, only the web content is reloaded. There's no way for the component to know the button shouldn't be there anymore.

We can fix this by manually removing the button when the Stimulus controller disconnects.[10] One way for disconnect() to be called is when the element's data-controller attribute is removed. And the page is refreshed when we sign out, removing the element.

Start by adding a disconnect() function in button_controller.js that sends the "disconnect" message to the app.

ch07_20/rails/app/javascript/controllers/bridge/button_controller.js
```
import { BridgeComponent } from "@hotwired/hotwire-native-bridge"

export default class extends BridgeComponent {
  static component = "button"

  connect() {
    // ...
  }

➤ disconnect() {
➤   super.disconnect()
➤
➤   this.send("disconnect")
➤ }
}
```

Back in ButtonComponent in Xcode, move the contents of onReceive(message:) to a new private function named connect(via:). Then, call this function only if the Message event is "connect".

ch07_21/ios/App/Components/ButtonComponent.swift
```
import HotwireNative
import UIKit

class ButtonComponent: BridgeComponent {
    override class var name: String { "button" }

    override func onReceive(message: Message) {
➤       if message.event == "connect" {
➤           connect(via: message)
➤       }
    }
```

---

10. https://stimulus.hotwired.dev/reference/lifecycle-callbacks#disconnection

```
    private func connect(via message: Message) {
        guard let data: MessageData = message.data() else { return }
        // ...
    }
}
// ...
```

Finally, add another private function called disconnect() that removes the button when the Message event is "disconnect".

ch07_22/ios/App/Components/ButtonComponent.swift
```
import HotwireNative
import UIKit

class ButtonComponent: BridgeComponent {
    override class var name: String { "button" }

    override func onReceive(message: Message) {
        if message.event == "connect" {
            connect(via: message)
        } else if message.event == "disconnect" {
            disconnect()
        }
    }

    private func connect(via message: Message) {
        // ...
    }

    private func disconnect() {
        let viewController = delegate?.destination as? UIViewController
        viewController?.navigationItem.rightBarButtonItem = nil
    }
}
// ...
```

Now, signing out will correctly remove the component.

I find myself often following these same steps when working with the native navigation bar. Cleaning up after ourselves is always a good idea. And here, we're preventing a subtle, but important, bug.

What's Next?

You now know how to build dynamic, server-powered bridge components for iOS. You know how to keep configuration in HTML, how to send messages, and how to reply back. You can use the same techniques to build your own components, taking advantage of any native API.

These bridge components provide a great compromise between web-only screens and native ones. They enable native interactions without fully investing in screens completely driven by SwiftUI. When built correctly, they can provide endless customization without new releases to the app stores—all that's required is changing some HTML.

If you're looking for more examples or inspiration, check out my open source bridge component library.[11] It includes a bunch of generalized, production-ready bridge components extracted from real-world client projects. Once configured, each component can be added to any page of your app and customized with a bit of HTML.

Up next, we'll build the same bridge component on Android. If you're only working on iOS right now, feel free to skip ahead to Chapter 9, Deploy to Physical Devices with TestFlight and Play Testing, on page 171, to learn how to get the app off of the simulator and into your hands.

---

11. https://github.com/joemasilotti/bridge-components

## CHAPTER 8

Build Android Bridge Components with Kotlin

In the previous chapter, you learned how to add bridge components to your iOS app. This chapter mirrors that for Android—you'll learn how to build a native button component to submit forms and navigate to new pages. Here's an example of what the sign-in screen will look like before (left) and after (right) working through this chapter:

A heads up that even if you're only working through the Android side of things, you'll still need to read through Chapter 7, Build iOS Bridge Components with Swift, on page 127. It introduces concepts and code that are required for building bridge components with Android. Don't forget to take advantage of the code checkpoint for starting this chapter, found in the ch08_00 directory.

The good news is that you'll reuse most of the JavaScript and Ruby code from the previous chapter. Here, you'll shift your focus to the Kotlin code because, well, there's a lot of it. You'll write close to 100 lines of Kotlin code in this chapter.

So, why do we need so much Kotlin when we accomplished the same on iOS with half as much Swift? The short answer is that Android can be much, much more verbose than iOS. And because its roots are Java-based, there are often additional layers of abstraction and configuration needed to do seemingly simple things.

But the magic of bridge components means you won't need to touch the native code to add the button to *new* pages. All that's required for that is a few lines of HTML markup with the right data-* attributes.

Following the same cadence as in the previous chapter, you'll start by creating a simple native component to ensure that everything is working as expected. You'll then progressively enhance it with more features, like dynamic text and an image, with the goal of making your hybrid app feel more native. And, as in the previous chapter, you'll keep the configuration on the server so the app remains flexible. Let's get to work!

Create a Native Component

Get started by opening Android Studio and creating a new package under com.masilotti.hikingjournal and name it components. Inside that package, create a new Kotlin file and name it ButtonComponent.

Inside this file, declare a BridgeComponent subclass named ButtonComponent.

ch08_01/android/app/src/main/java/com/masilotti/hikingjournal/components/ButtonComponent.kt
```
package com.masilotti.hikingjournal.components

import dev.hotwire.core.bridge.BridgeComponent
import dev.hotwire.core.bridge.BridgeDelegate
import dev.hotwire.navigation.destinations.HotwireDestination

class ButtonComponent(
    name: String,
    private val bridgeDelegate: BridgeDelegate<HotwireDestination>
) : BridgeComponent<HotwireDestination>(name, bridgeDelegate) {
}
```

Excluding the package and import statements, these five lines of code can be pretty intimidating. Coming from Ruby, I had no idea what was going on the first time I saw them! Let's break it down.

ButtonComponent inherits from BridgeComponent, signified by the colon. This isn't any different than what you did when you made MapFragment inherit from

HotwireFragment in Chapter 6, Render Native Screens with Jetpack Compose, on page 103.

```
class MapFragment : HotwireFragment() {
  // ...
}
```

The tricky part is that BridgeComponent has two required parameters to be instantiated: name and bridgeDelegate. Hence, these parameters appear between the *second* set of parentheses. They're passed from the ButtonComponent's initializer in the *first* set of parentheses. This means that when a ButtonComponent is created, it will automatically pass those parameters to its superclass, Bridge-Component.

Finally, adding private val in front of the bridgeDelegate property creates an immutable instance variable for us to access *inside* of ButtonComponent. You'll use this to grab a reference to the Fragment that's rendering the component.

In Ruby, this could look like the following:

```
class ButtonComponent < BridgeComponent
  attr_reader :bridge_delegate
  private :bridge_delegate

  def initialize(name, bridge_delegate)
    @bridge_delegate = bridge_delegate
    super(name, bridge_delegate)
  end
end

class BridgeComponent
  def initialize(name, bridge_delegate)
    # ...
  end
end
```

You might have noticed that this code isn't compiling yet. Move your cursor over the red squiggled ButtonComponent and press ⌥ ↵. Click Implement members and then click OK. This will add an unimplemented, but required, onReceive(message: Message) function. I bet you can tell what that's used for—you used a function of the same name in the previous chapter, on iOS, to handle received messages received over the bridge.

ch08_02/android/app/src/main/java/com/masilotti/hikingjournal/components/ButtonComponent.kt
```
package com.masilotti.hikingjournal.components

import dev.hotwire.core.bridge.BridgeComponent
import dev.hotwire.core.bridge.BridgeDelegate
import dev.hotwire.core.bridge.Message
import dev.hotwire.navigation.destinations.HotwireDestination
```

```kotlin
class ButtonComponent(
    name: String,
    private val bridgeDelegate: BridgeDelegate<HotwireDestination>
) : BridgeComponent<HotwireDestination>(name, bridgeDelegate) {
    override fun onReceive(message: Message) {
        TODO("Not yet implemented")
    }
}
```

Next, you need to make Hotwire Native aware of the component. You won't instantiate bridge components directly; Hotwire Native will do it for us. Open HikingJournalApplication and register ButtonComponent with the name "button", which aligns it with the value of component on the JavaScript side of things.

ch08_03/android/app/src/main/java/com/masilotti/hikingjournal/HikingJournalApplication.kt
```kotlin
package com.masilotti.hikingjournal

import android.app.Application
import com.masilotti.hikingjournal.activities.baseURL
import com.masilotti.hikingjournal.components.ButtonComponent
import com.masilotti.hikingjournal.fragments.MapFragment
import dev.hotwire.core.bridge.BridgeComponentFactory
import dev.hotwire.core.config.Hotwire
import dev.hotwire.core.turbo.config.PathConfiguration
import dev.hotwire.navigation.config.registerBridgeComponents
import dev.hotwire.navigation.config.registerFragmentDestinations
import dev.hotwire.navigation.fragments.HotwireWebFragment

class HikingJournalApplication : Application() {
    override fun onCreate() {
        // ...

        Hotwire.registerFragmentDestinations(
            // ...
        )

        Hotwire.registerBridgeComponents(
            BridgeComponentFactory("button", ::ButtonComponent)
        )
    }
}
```

And yes, those two leading colons are intentional! That's Kotlin's way of referencing a class, like in Swift when we used ButtonComponent.self.

You'll use Compose to render the contents of the component. And just like in When to Go Native, on page 81, you'll do that with a ComposeView. But each ComposeView needs a hook to bridge the gap between Jetpack Compose and the traditional Android View system.

We'll use the HotwireFragment from Hotwire Native as our bridge. And we can grab a reference to it by casting BridgeDelegate in ButtonComponent.

ch08_04/android/app/src/main/java/com/masilotti/hikingjournal/components/ButtonComponent.kt
```
package com.masilotti.hikingjournal.components

import dev.hotwire.core.bridge.BridgeComponent
import dev.hotwire.core.bridge.BridgeDelegate
import dev.hotwire.core.bridge.Message
import dev.hotwire.navigation.destinations.HotwireDestination
➤ import dev.hotwire.navigation.fragments.HotwireFragment

class ButtonComponent(
    name: String,
    private val bridgeDelegate: BridgeDelegate<HotwireDestination>
) : BridgeComponent<HotwireDestination>(name, bridgeDelegate) {
➤    private val fragment: HotwireFragment
➤        get() = bridgeDelegate.destination.fragment as HotwireFragment

    override fun onReceive(message: Message) {
        TODO("Not yet implemented")
    }
}
```

Next, create the ComposeView and use setContent() to render a Text() element with static text.

ch08_05/android/app/src/main/java/com/masilotti/hikingjournal/components/ButtonComponent.kt
```
package com.masilotti.hikingjournal.components

➤ import androidx.compose.material3.Text
➤ import androidx.compose.ui.platform.ComposeView
import dev.hotwire.core.bridge.BridgeComponent
import dev.hotwire.core.bridge.BridgeDelegate
import dev.hotwire.core.bridge.Message
import dev.hotwire.navigation.destinations.HotwireDestination
import dev.hotwire.navigation.fragments.HotwireFragment

class ButtonComponent(
    name: String,
    private val bridgeDelegate: BridgeDelegate<HotwireDestination>
) : BridgeComponent<HotwireDestination>(name, bridgeDelegate) {
    private val fragment: HotwireFragment
        get() = bridgeDelegate.destination.fragment as HotwireFragment

    override fun onReceive(message: Message) {
➤        val composeView = ComposeView(fragment.requireContext()).apply {
➤            setContent {
➤                Text("Sign in")
➤            }
➤        }
    }
}
```

Add the `ComposeView` to the screen by attaching it to the `Toolbar`. Remember, you've cast the fragment property to an instance of HotwireFragment. This provides you with the convenient toolbarForNavigation(), referencing the existing toolbar (provided by Hotwire Native) at the top of the screen.

ch08_06/android/app/src/main/java/com/masilotti/hikingjournal/components/ButtonComponent.kt
```
// ...

class ButtonComponent(
    name: String,
    private val bridgeDelegate: BridgeDelegate<HotwireDestination>
) : BridgeComponent<HotwireDestination>(name, bridgeDelegate) {
    private val fragment: HotwireFragment
        get() = bridgeDelegate.destination.fragment as HotwireFragment

    override fun onReceive(message: Message) {
        val composeView = ComposeView(fragment.requireContext()).apply {
            // ...
        }

        val toolbar = fragment.toolbarForNavigation()
        toolbar?.addView(composeView)
    }
}
```

This is a good spot to stop and check your work, so go ahead and run the app. If you're not signed in, tap the Sign in button at the bottom of the screen. You'll then see the native Sign in button (yay!). But it's pushed all the way to the left (boo!).

Align the button by applying Toolbar.LayoutParams with Gravity.END to push it to the right and pass it to addView().

ch08_07/android/app/src/main/java/com/masilotti/hikingjournal/components/ButtonComponent.kt
```
package com.masilotti.hikingjournal.components

import android.view.Gravity
import android.view.ViewGroup
import androidx.appcompat.widget.Toolbar
import androidx.compose.material3.Text
```

```
import androidx.compose.ui.platform.ComposeView
// ...

class ButtonComponent(
    name: String,
    private val bridgeDelegate: BridgeDelegate<HotwireDestination>
) : BridgeComponent<HotwireDestination>(name, bridgeDelegate) {
    private val fragment: HotwireFragment
        get() = bridgeDelegate.destination.fragment as HotwireFragment

    override fun onReceive(message: Message) {
        val composeView = ComposeView(fragment.requireContext()).apply {
            // ...
        }
        val layoutParams = Toolbar.LayoutParams(
            ViewGroup.LayoutParams.WRAP_CONTENT,
            ViewGroup.LayoutParams.WRAP_CONTENT
        ).apply { gravity = Gravity.END }

        val toolbar = fragment.toolbarForNavigation()
        toolbar?.addView(composeView, layoutParams)
    }
}
```

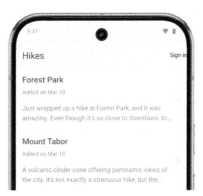

Better! The button is now aligned to the right. But perhaps a little *too* far; it could use some room to breathe. When you convert this Text() to a real Button(), it will automatically add some padding. Let's do that next.

Respond to Button Taps

To convert our text to a tappable button, replace the contents of setContent with a Button().

ch08_08/android/app/src/main/java/com/masilotti/hikingjournal/components/ButtonComponent.kt
```
// ...
import android.view.Gravity
import android.view.ViewGroup
import androidx.appcompat.widget.Toolbar
import androidx.compose.material3.Button
```

```kotlin
import androidx.compose.material3.Text
import androidx.compose.ui.platform.ComposeView
// ...

class ButtonComponent(
    name: String,
    private val bridgeDelegate: BridgeDelegate<HotwireDestination>
) : BridgeComponent<HotwireDestination>(name, bridgeDelegate) {
    private val fragment: HotwireFragment
        get() = bridgeDelegate.destination.fragment as HotwireFragment

    override fun onReceive(message: Message) {
        val composeView = ComposeView(fragment.requireContext()).apply {
            setContent {
                Button(
                    onClick = { replyTo(message.event) }
                ) {
                    Text("Sign in")
                }
            }
        }
        // ...
    }
}
```

When the button is tapped, it will call the code you assigned to onClick. As you did in the previous chapter, replying to message.event tells the corresponding JavaScript code to click the web-based button.

Go ahead and run the app and click Sign in. You'll see a big purple button in the upper right.

But there's an odd bug. Dismiss the sign-in screen by tapping the X in the upper left. Then, tap Sign in again. Now, there are multiple buttons, as shown in the screenshot on page 157.

Every time you visit a page with this bridge component, a *new* button is added to the screen. On iOS, you *set* the button via rightBarButtonItem =, so you didn't

have this problem. But on Android, `toolbar?.addView()` adds a new one each time the screen loads. Let's fix that before moving on.

Remove Duplicate Buttons

Start by moving everything inside of `onReceive(message: Message)` to a new private function named `addButton(message: Message)`.

ch08_09/android/app/src/main/java/com/masilotti/hikingjournal/components/ButtonComponent.kt
```
// ...

class ButtonComponent(
    name: String,
    private val bridgeDelegate: BridgeDelegate<HotwireDestination>
) : BridgeComponent<HotwireDestination>(name, bridgeDelegate) {
    private val fragment: HotwireFragment
        get() = bridgeDelegate.destination.fragment as HotwireFragment

    override fun onReceive(message: Message) {
        addButton(message)
    }

    private fun addButton(message: Message) {
        val composeView = ComposeView(fragment.requireContext()).apply {
            // ...
        }
        // ...
    }
}
```

Then, set an `id` on the button. The value itself is arbitrary; it could be anything. You just need a reference for finding it later. Here, I've set the value to 1.

ch08_10/android/app/src/main/java/com/masilotti/hikingjournal/components/ButtonComponent.kt
```
// ...

class ButtonComponent(
    name: String,
    private val bridgeDelegate: BridgeDelegate<HotwireDestination>
) : BridgeComponent<HotwireDestination>(name, bridgeDelegate) {
```

```
    private val buttonId = 1
    private val fragment: HotwireFragment
        get() = bridgeDelegate.destination.fragment as HotwireFragment

    // ...

    private fun addButton(message: Message) {
        val composeView = ComposeView(fragment.requireContext()).apply {
            id = buttonId
            setContent {
                Button(
                    onClick = { replyTo(message.event) }
                ) {
                    Text("Sign in")
                }
            }
        }
        // ...
    }
}
```

Add a private function to remove the button from the toolbar via findViewById(),
passing in the id set previously.

ch08_11/android/app/src/main/java/com/masilotti/hikingjournal/components/ButtonComponent.kt
```
// ...

class ButtonComponent(
    name: String,
    private val bridgeDelegate: BridgeDelegate<HotwireDestination>
) : BridgeComponent<HotwireDestination>(name, bridgeDelegate) {
    private val buttonId = 1
    private val fragment: HotwireFragment
        get() = bridgeDelegate.destination.fragment as HotwireFragment

    override fun onReceive(message: Message) {
        addButton(message)
    }

    private fun addButton(message: Message) {
        // ...
    }

    private fun removeButton() {
        val toolbar = fragment.toolbarForNavigation()
        val button = toolbar?.findViewById<ComposeView>(buttonId)
        toolbar?.removeView(button)
    }
}
```

Back in onReceive(message: Message), only add the button when the event name
is "connect" and remove it on "disconnect". Also, remove it before adding it
(again) just in case there's already one there. This ensures the button gets

removed every time the screen disappears, mimicking the pattern you built on iOS.

ch08_12/android/app/src/main/java/com/masilotti/hikingjournal/components/ButtonComponent.kt
```kotlin
// ...

class ButtonComponent(
    name: String,
    private val bridgeDelegate: BridgeDelegate<HotwireDestination>
) : BridgeComponent<HotwireDestination>(name, bridgeDelegate) {
    private val buttonId = 1
    private val fragment: HotwireFragment
        get() = bridgeDelegate.destination.fragment as HotwireFragment

    override fun onReceive(message: Message) {
➤        if (message.event == "connect") {
➤            removeButton()
➤            addButton(message)
➤        } else if (message.event == "disconnect") {
➤            removeButton()
➤        }
    }

    // ...
}
```

Bug: fixed. Let's refactor a bit. When I build Compose views, I like to keep them self-contained as much as possible. So let's extract the button code to a @Composable function, as you did in Build a Compose View, on page 107. Pass in the button title so you can easily make it dynamic later.

ch08_13/android/app/src/main/java/com/masilotti/hikingjournal/components/ButtonComponent.kt
```kotlin
// ...
import androidx.compose.material3.Button
import androidx.compose.material3.Text
➤ import androidx.compose.runtime.Composable
import androidx.compose.ui.platform.ComposeView
import dev.hotwire.core.bridge.BridgeComponent
// ...

class ButtonComponent(
    name: String,
    private val bridgeDelegate: BridgeDelegate<HotwireDestination>
) : BridgeComponent<HotwireDestination>(name, bridgeDelegate) {
    // ...

    private fun addButton(message: Message) {
        val composeView = ComposeView(fragment.requireContext()).apply {
            id = buttonId
            setContent {
➤                ToolbarButton(
➤                    title = "Sign in",
➤                    onClick = { replyTo(message.event) }
```

```
                    )
                }
            }
            // ...
        }
        // ...
    }

@Composable
private fun ToolbarButton(title: String, onClick: () -> Unit) {
    Button(
        onClick = onClick
    ) {
        Text(title)
    }
}
```

While you're in here, clean up the design of the button a bit. The following code will remove the purple background and make the text black, matching the title.

ch08_14/android/app/src/main/java/com/masilotti/hikingjournal/components/ButtonComponent.kt

```
// ...
import androidx.compose.material3.Button
import androidx.compose.material3.Text
import androidx.compose.material3.ButtonDefaults
import androidx.compose.runtime.Composable
import androidx.compose.ui.graphics.Color
import androidx.compose.ui.platform.ComposeView
import dev.hotwire.core.bridge.BridgeComponent
// ...

class ButtonComponent(
    name: String,
    private val bridgeDelegate: BridgeDelegate<HotwireDestination>
) : BridgeComponent<HotwireDestination>(name, bridgeDelegate) {
    // ...
}

@Composable
private fun ToolbarButton(title: String, onClick: () -> Unit) {
    Button(
        onClick = onClick,
        colors = ButtonDefaults.buttonColors(
            containerColor = Color.Transparent,
            contentColor = Color.Black
        )
    ) {
        Text(title)
    }
}
```

Looking good! The button now matches the system UI and feels at home for Android users.

Up next, you'll make the button text dynamic so you can use it for more than simply signing in. Think: an Add button on the hikes index page to add a new hike and a Save button when editing a hike to submit the form.

Make the Button Text Dynamic

The title of the button is coming in via JSON from the bridge component on the web. And to parse JSON on Android, you need to configure a serialization library.[1]

Start by adding the library to the module's build.gradle.kts—once to the plugins section and again at the bottom to the dependencies section.

```
ch08_15/android/app/build.gradle.kts
plugins {
    alias(libs.plugins.android.application)
    alias(libs.plugins.kotlin.android)
    alias(libs.plugins.compose.compiler)
    id("com.google.android.libraries.mapsplatform.secrets-gradle-plugin")
    id("org.jetbrains.kotlin.plugin.serialization")
}

// ...

dependencies {
    // ...
    implementation("androidx.compose.ui:ui-tooling-preview")
    implementation("com.google.maps.android:maps-compose:6.1.0")
    implementation("org.jetbrains.kotlinx:kotlinx-serialization-json:1.8.1")
    debugImplementation("androidx.compose.ui:ui-tooling")
    testImplementation(libs.junit)
    androidTestImplementation(libs.androidx.junit)
    androidTestImplementation(libs.androidx.espresso.core)
}
```

---

1. https://kotlinlang.org/docs/serialization.html

Then, add the plugin to the top-level build.gradle.kts file and sync Gradle.

ch08_15/android/build.gradle.kts
```
// Top-level build file where you can add configuration options common to all
// sub-projects/modules.
plugins {
    alias(libs.plugins.android.application) apply false
    alias(libs.plugins.kotlin.android) apply false
    alias(libs.plugins.compose.compiler) apply false
    id("org.jetbrains.kotlin.plugin.serialization") version "2.0.0" apply false
}

buildscript {
    dependencies {
        classpath(
            "com.google.android.libraries.mapsplatform" +
                    ".secrets-gradle-plugin:secrets-gradle-plugin:2.0.1"
        )
    }
}
```

Finally, tell Hotwire Native which library you're using by setting jsonConverter in HikingJournalApplication.

ch08_15/android/app/src/main/java/com/masilotti/hikingjournal/HikingJournalApplication.kt
```
// ...
import com.masilotti.hikingjournal.fragments.MapFragment
import dev.hotwire.core.bridge.BridgeComponentFactory
import dev.hotwire.core.bridge.KotlinXJsonConverter
import dev.hotwire.core.config.Hotwire
import dev.hotwire.core.turbo.config.PathConfiguration
// ...

class HikingJournalApplication : Application() {
    override fun onCreate() {
        // ...

        Hotwire.registerBridgeComponents(
            BridgeComponentFactory("button", ::ButtonComponent)
        )

        Hotwire.config.jsonConverter = KotlinXJsonConverter()
    }
}
```

With your serializer configured, you can now set up a data class to serialize. This will map the JSON payload to a Kotlin object that you can then read in your code.

Back in ButtonComponent, create a MessageData class that parses "title" to a String value.

ch08_16/android/app/src/main/java/com/masilotti/hikingjournal/components/ButtonComponent.kt

```
// ...
import dev.hotwire.navigation.destinations.HotwireDestination
import dev.hotwire.navigation.fragments.HotwireFragment
➤ import kotlinx.serialization.SerialName
➤ import kotlinx.serialization.Serializable

class ButtonComponent(
    name: String,
    private val bridgeDelegate: BridgeDelegate<HotwireDestination>
) : BridgeComponent<HotwireDestination>(name, bridgeDelegate) {
    // ...
}

@Composable
private fun ToolbarButton(title: String, onClick: () -> Unit) {
    // ...
}

➤ @Serializable
➤ data class MessageData(
➤     @SerialName("title") val title: String
➤ )
```

Then, extract data from the Message at the top of addButton(message: Message),
passing the title to the constructor of ToolbarButton.

ch08_17/android/app/src/main/java/com/masilotti/hikingjournal/components/ButtonComponent.kt

```
// ...
class ButtonComponent(
    name: String,
    private val bridgeDelegate: BridgeDelegate<HotwireDestination>
) : BridgeComponent<HotwireDestination>(name, bridgeDelegate) {
    // ...

    private fun addButton(message: Message) {
➤       val data = message.data<MessageData>() ?: return

        val composeView = ComposeView(fragment.requireContext()).apply {
            id = buttonId
            setContent {
                ToolbarButton(
➤                   title = data.title,
                    onClick = { replyTo(message.event) }
                )
            }
        }
        // ...
    }
    // ...
}
// ...
```

Here the ?: operator, or the Elvis Operator,[2] only calls return if message.data<MessageData>() returns null. This is Kotlin's equivalent of a guard statement like you used on iOS.

Run the app and sign in. You'll see the Add and Save buttons correctly labeled, pulling in dynamic data that you set in the HTML in the previous chapter.

OK, just one more step to get feature parity with iOS: add a dynamic image.

Add a Dynamic Image

The names of icons are different on iOS and Android. So, to keep the meaning of these icons consistent, we need a way to uniquely differentiate one from another.

Start by opening button_controller.js in the Rails app and update the reference to the iOS icon to distinguish it from an Android one. Then, add a second value for Android.

ch08_18/rails/app/javascript/controllers/bridge/button_controller.js
```
import { BridgeComponent } from "@hotwired/hotwire-native-bridge"

export default class extends BridgeComponent {
  static component = "button"

  connect() {
    super.connect()

    const title = this.bridgeElement.bridgeAttribute("title")
    const imageName = this.bridgeElement.bridgeAttribute("ios-image-name")
    const iconName = this.bridgeElement.bridgeAttribute("android-icon-name")
    this.send("connect", {title, imageName, iconName}, () => {
      this.bridgeElement.click()
    })
  }
}
```

---

2.   https://kotlinlang.org/docs/null-safety.html#elvis-operator

```
  disconnect() {
    super.disconnect()

    this.send("disconnect")
  }
}
```

This lets us use data-bridge-ios-image-name to set the iOS image name and data-bridge-android-icon-name to set the Android image name. And because you kept imageName the same (you only *added* iconName), you don't need to go back and update the native iOS code.

Apply these changes to the HTML by opening the hikes index page and adding the new data attribute for the Android icon.

ch08_18/rails/app/views/hikes/index.html.erb
```erb
<%# ... %>

<div class="container d-flex justify-content-between gap-2 mt-4">
  <% if user_signed_in? %>
    <%= link_to "Add a hike", new_hike_path,
      class: "btn btn-primary flex-grow-1 flex-sm-grow-0", data: {
        controller: "bridge--button",
        bridge_title: "Add",
        bridge_ios_image_name: "plus",
        bridge_android_icon_name: "add"
      } %>
    <%# ... %>
  <% else %>
    <%# ... %>
  <% end %>
</div>
```

And do the same on the hikes show page.

ch08_18/rails/app/views/hikes/show.html.erb
```erb
<%= render "shared/header", title: @hike.name %>

<div class="container">
  <%# ... %>

  <div class="d-flex align-items-center mt-3">
    <%= render "likes/like", hike: @hike, like: @like %>

    <div class="d-flex gap-2 ms-auto">
      <%# ... %>

      <% if user_signed_in? && @hike.user == current_user %>
        <%= link_to edit_hike_path(@hike), class: "btn btn-outline-primary",
          data: {
            controller: "bridge--button",
            bridge_title: "Edit",
            bridge_ios_image_name: "pencil",
            bridge_android_icon_name: "edit"
```

```
        } do %>
        <i class="bi bi-pencil"></i>
        Edit
      <% end %>
    <% end %>
  </div>
</div>

<%# ... %>
</div>
```

Next, you'll extract this new value and use it to set an icon on the button.

Remember how in Add a Dynamic Image, on page 142, you sent a String directly to UIImage(systemName:) and iOS turned it into an image from SF Symbols? Well, we can't do exactly that on Android. Image resources on Android need to be statically bundled with the app—anything we want to use needs to be shipped when we deploy. Since there's no SF Symbols equivalent on Android, we'll bundle a custom font that includes all of the available Material Symbols. Kind of like a sprite sheet in game development!

Head to the Google Fonts icons page[3] to download the font. Make sure Material Symbols (new) is selected on the left. Then, scroll through the options at the top to the right and click Download Material Symbols.

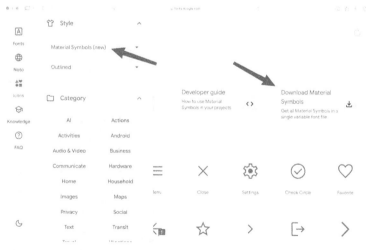

The downloaded zip file contains three fonts, but we only need one. Open the Material_Symbols_Outlined folder and rename the .ttf font file to material_symbols.ttf. We'll add this font to our project in Android Studio.

---

3.   https://fonts.google.com/icons

In Android Studio, create a new resource directory for fonts. Right-click the res directory on the left and select New -> Android Resource Directory. Select font from the Resource type dropdown and click OK.

Drag and drop the .ttf font file to this directory. Select Refactor in the dialog for Android Studio to move the file into the project.

OK, back to Kotlin. Pop back open ButtonComponent, and let's render an image.

Add a second property to MessageData to parse "iconName" as a String. Then, add a new parameter to ToolbarButton() to pass in this value. Don't forget to update the calling code in addButton(), too.

ch08_19/android/app/src/main/java/com/masilotti/hikingjournal/components/ButtonComponent.kt

```kotlin
// ...

class ButtonComponent(
    name: String,
    private val bridgeDelegate: BridgeDelegate<HotwireDestination>
) : BridgeComponent<HotwireDestination>(name, bridgeDelegate) {
    // ...
    private fun addButton(message: Message) {
        val data = message.data<MessageData>() ?: return

        val composeView = ComposeView(fragment.requireContext()).apply {
            id = buttonId
            setContent {
                ToolbarButton(
                    title = data.title,
                    iconName = data.iconName,
                    onClick = { replyTo(message.event) }
                )
            }
        }
        // ...
    }
    // ...
}

@Composable
private fun ToolbarButton(
```

```
➤        title: String,
➤        iconName: String?,
➤        onClick: () -> Unit
➤    ) {
         // ...
     }

     @Serializable
     data class MessageData(
➤        @SerialName("title") val title: String,
➤        @SerialName("iconName") val iconName: String?
     )
```

Then, in the @Composable, replace the body of Button() with Text(). By using the liga font feature, we can render images directly from the font file. Use the ?: operator to fall back to Text when an icon isn't given.

ch08_20/android/app/src/main/java/com/masilotti/hikingjournal/components/ButtonComponent.kt

```
     // ...
     import androidx.compose.ui.graphics.Color
     import androidx.compose.ui.platform.ComposeView
➤    import androidx.compose.ui.text.TextStyle
➤    import androidx.compose.ui.text.font.Font
➤    import androidx.compose.ui.text.font.FontFamily
➤    import androidx.compose.ui.unit.sp
➤    import com.masilotti.hikingjournal.R
     import dev.hotwire.core.bridge.BridgeComponent
     import dev.hotwire.core.bridge.BridgeDelegate
     // ...

     class ButtonComponent(
         name: String,
         private val bridgeDelegate: BridgeDelegate<HotwireDestination>
     ) : BridgeComponent<HotwireDestination>(name, bridgeDelegate) {
         // ...
     }

     @Composable
     private fun ToolbarButton(
         title: String,
         iconName: String?,
         onClick: () -> Unit
     ) {
         Button(
             onClick = onClick,
             colors = ButtonDefaults.buttonColors(
                 containerColor = Color.Transparent,
                 contentColor = Color.Black
             )
         ) {
➤            iconName?.let {
➤                Text(
```

```
➤          text = it,
➤          fontFamily = FontFamily(Font(R.font.material_symbols)),
➤          fontSize = 28.sp,
➤          style = TextStyle(fontFeatureSettings = "liga")
➤        )
➤    } ?: Text(title)
  }
}

// ...
```

These image names can be found for each icon back on the Google Fonts page, under Icon name when selecting an icon.

Run the app and sign in. You'll see the Add button replaced with a nice little plus sign. And when you visit a hike page, a pencil will replace the Edit button.

Phew! Take a moment to reflect on the code you wrote—almost 100 new lines of Kotlin. With this and the previous chapter's code in place, you can add native buttons to any screen in the app, all without changing a single line of Swift *or* Kotlin.

What's Next?

You now know how to build dynamic, server-powered bridge components for Android. Adding a new native button is now as easy as adding one or two data-* attributes to your HTML. And because you made the title and image dynamic, your options for customization are endless.

You can follow the technique you learned in this chapter to build your own components, taking advantage of any native API. Swap out the code in onClick to execute whatever Kotlin you'd like, such as accessing the Health Platform API,[4] interacting with the device's sensors,[5] and more.

If you're looking for more examples or inspiration, check out my open source bridge component library.[6] It includes a bunch of generalized, production-ready bridge components extracted from real-world client projects. Once configured, each component can be added to any page of your app and customized with a bit of HTML.

With bridge components done, your app is almost feature-complete! All that's left is adding push notifications in Chapter 10, Send Push Notifications with APNs and FCM, on page 195. But to do that, we first need to register our apps with Apple and Google to use their push notification services.

In the next chapter, you'll learn how to get your app off the emulator and onto a real device. We'll set up the app on App Store Connect and the Google Play Console, package a build in Xcode and Android Studio, and then deploy it with TestFlight and Google Play Testing. And the best part? You can invite your friends and colleagues to download the app and show them what you've been working on.

---

4. https://developer.android.com/health-and-fitness/guides/health-services/health-platform
5. https://developer.android.com/reference/android/hardware/SensorManager
6. https://github.com/joemasilotti/bridge-components

## CHAPTER 9

Deploy to Physical Devices with TestFlight and Play Testing

By now, you have a solid understanding of how to build iOS and Android apps powered by Hotwire Native. You can add a native tab bar, render views with SwiftUI and Jetpack Compose, and progressively enhance screens with bridge components. But, if you build an app and never deploy it...is it really an app? And if you don't deploy your app, there's no way to show off your hard work to your friends and colleagues!

Testing on a *real* device is a prerequisite for deployment. This chapter walks you through getting your apps on real, physical devices. You'll deploy the iOS app with TestFlight, a first-party app from Apple that lets folks download apps for beta testing before they arrive in the App Store. You'll then use Google Play Testing to get the Android app off of the emulator and into your hands for beta testing.

For iOS, you'll work through these steps:

1. Set up your app in App Store Connect.
2. Archive a build in Xcode.
3. Download the app to your device via TestFlight.

Let's get started.

Add an App to App Store Connect

App Store apps are managed through App Store Connect.[1] You'll use this to upload builds, submit apps, review analytics, and more. To get started, you'll need to join the Apple Developer Program.

Join the Apple Developer Program

Visit the Apple Developer Program[2] landing page and start your enrollment. A heads up that you'll need an Apple account with two-factor authentication enabled to register. Choose between an Individual or Organization account based on the program guidelines.

And yes, the Apple Developer Program costs $99 per year. The good news is that this comes with code-level support,[3] provided directly by developers at Apple. I've used this in the past to ask very specific questions about an app I was building and was pleasantly surprised at the level of feedback I received. It's a great resource for developers new to iOS.

Once you have an account, you can configure the app and its identifier.

Create an App Identifier

Every app has a unique identifier in the App Store. To get yours on TestFlight, you need to first register an app identifier with Apple.

To create an app identifier, sign in to the Apple Developer[4] portal and click the Account button in the upper right. I recommend bookmarking this page—it has a few handy links you'll continue to come back to as you launch iOS apps in the App Store.

Then, from the Certificates, IDs & Profiles section, click Identifiers, as shown in the first screenshot on page 173.

On the next screen, click the blue plus sign next to Identifiers. Make sure App IDs is selected, and click Continue. Ensure that App is selected, and click Continue again.

Fill in the Description field with something to remember the identifier by. Don't stress about this descriptor; it's never shown externally. I usually set

---

1. https://developer.apple.com/app-store-connect/
2. https://developer.apple.com/programs/enroll/
3. https://developer.apple.com/support/technical/
4. https://developer.apple.com

it to the name of my app plus "app identifier." Then, populate Bundle ID with the *bundle identifier* of the app. Click Continue and then Register.

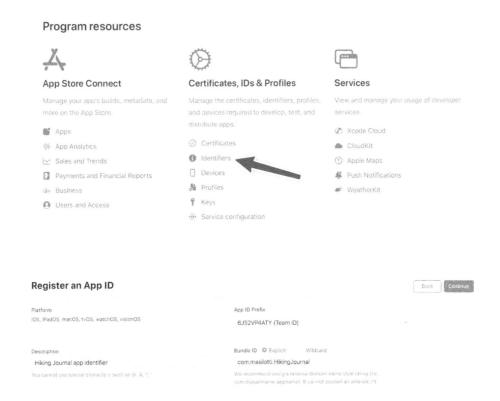

When we first created the Xcode project in Chapter 1, Build Your First Hotwire Native Apps, on page 1, we set an organization identifier of "com.masilotti" and an app name of "HikingJournal." Xcode used this to generate our bundle identifier of "com.masilotti.HikingJournal". If you changed your bundle identifier via the field shown in the screenshot on page 174, then make sure to reflect that in the Bundle ID field in the web form before continuing.

With your identifier in hand, you can configure the app on App Store Connect.

Configure a New App

Start by visiting App Store Connect[5] and clicking the big blue Apps button (if you aren't automatically redirected). If you don't want to remember another URL, this is linked from the Apple Developer portal I mentioned bookmarking earlier.

---

5.   https://appstoreconnect.apple.com

Next, click the blue plus button next to Apps at the top. Select New App from the dropdown.

On the next screen, shown on page 175, populate the fields with the following and click Create. Like before, make sure to update Bundle ID if you changed yours.

- *Platforms*: iOS
- *Name*: Hiking Journal
- *Primary Language*: English (U.S.)
- *Bundle ID*: Hiking Journal—com.masilotti.HikingJournal
- *SKU*: com.masilotti.HikingJournal
- *User Access*: Full Access

Apple is now officially aware of your new app. High five! With that in place, you can start uploading builds for distribution.

Archive and Upload a Build

Back in Xcode, click Product → Archive from the Menu Bar. This creates a binary with the metadata of your code that you can upload to App Store Connect.

New App

Platforms ?
☑ iOS   macOS   tvOS   visionOS

Name ?

Hiking Journal

Primary Language ?

English (U.S.)   ⌄

Bundle ID ?

Hiking Journal - com.masilotti.HikingJournal   ⌄

SKU ?

com.masilotti.HikingJournal

User Access ?
    Limited Access   ◉ Full Access

After a few moments, Xcode will let you know that the build failed with the following error message:

> Signing for "HikingJournal" requires a development team. Select a development team in the Signing & Capabilities editor.

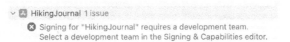

For Apple to verify this archive is indeed your code, you need to sign the build. Think of this as a signed commit on GitHub—an extra layer of security to protect your codebase.

Click the HikingJournal project from the Project Navigator on the left, select HikingJournal from TARGETS (not PROJECT) in the middle column, and then select the Signing & Capabilities tab at the top.

If you haven't signed in to your account in Xcode yet, you'll see a button titled Add Account.... Click that and sign in with your Apple Developer account, as shown in the first screenshot on page 176.

After signing in, select the team from the Team dropdown that replaced the Add Account... button, as shown in the second screenshot on page 176.

The checkbox labeled "Automatically manage signing" will do all the hard work of downloading and signing certificates and provisioning profiles for you. I highly recommend you let Xcode do this for you.

Archive the app again via Product → Archive from the Menu Bar. It works this time!

The Archives window will pop up, listing all the archives you've made of this app. For now, there's only one in there. Select it and click Distribute App on the right. On the next screen, select App Store Connect and then click Distribute, as shown in the first screenshot on page 177.

Sadly, the upload fails with an error message complaining that CFBundleIconName is missing, as shown in the second screenshot on page 177. We need an app icon to upload builds to App Store Connect. Close this dialog and do just that.

Add an App Icon

Open Assets under the Resources folder. Click AppIcon from the middle column—notice there's nothing there, as shown in the third screenshot on page 177. We need a 1024x1024 pixel image.

I've included an example app icon along with the book's source code. Navigate to the assets directory next to the chapter checkpoints. Inside, you will find AppIcon.png. Click and drag that file over the dotted outline in Xcode to apply the image. Xcode will automatically copy it to the correct location and bundle it with your app.

Upload a new build with the app icon by archiving the app, selecting it from the Organizer, and clicking Distribute App. Success!

HikingJournal 1.0 (1) uploaded
Show in App Store Connect

Once the build uploads, it needs to process before you can distribute it. Check its progress by clicking the little gray arrow or by visiting App Store Connect.[6] Builds show up in the TestFlight tab after selecting the app.

Verify the Build on App Store Connect

Once the build finishes processing, you'll see the app icon and a warning triangle under the Status column. You're required to declare what type of encryption your app uses before it can be distributed. Click the Manage link next to Missing Compliance to resolve this.

Since your app doesn't use encryption, you can select the last option from the dialog ("None of the algorithms mentioned above") and click Save, as shown in the screenshot on page 179.

---

6.   https://appstoreconnect.apple.com

App Encryption Documentation

What type of encryption algorithms does your app implement?

 Encryption algorithms that are proprietary or not accepted as standard by international standard bodies (IEEE, IETF, ITU, etc.)

Standard encryption algorithms instead of, or in addition to, using or accessing the encryption within Apple's operating system

Both algorithms mentioned above

None of the algorithms mentioned above

To bypass setting up export compliance in App Store Connect, you can specify your use of encryption directly in the information property list (Info.plist) in your Xcode project. If you need to provide documentation, Apple will provide you with a key value to add to the Info.plist. Learn More

---

Speed Up Future Builds

 You'll need to manually select this encryption option from App Store Connect for every build you upload. You can speed up future builds by adding <key>ITSAppUsesNonExemptEncryption</key><false/> to Info.plist under the Resources folder in Xcode. More information can be found from the Learn More[7] link in the dialog above.

The build is ready. Next, you need to tell App Store Connect who to distribute it to.

Create an Internal Testing Group

From the left column, click the blue plus sign next to INTERNAL TESTING.

Name this group "Internal Testers" and make sure the "Enable automatic distribution" option is checked. This ensures that every time a build uploads, each tester in the group gets a notification to download the latest release. Click Create.

Create New Internal Group

You can add up to 100 testers, and they can test builds using the TestFlight app.

> Internal Testers

Select the "Enable automatic distribution" checkbox to automatically deliver all Xcode builds to everyone in the group. Xcode Cloud builds have to be added manually. This setting cannot be updated later.

☑ Enable automatic distribution

7.　https://developer.apple.com/documentation/security/complying_with_encryption_export_regulations

You can only have up to 100 internal testers,[8] but builds distributed to these folks do *not* have to go through manual review from Apple. So, you are free to upload often and create a quick feedback cycle. If you want to distribute to more than 100 testers, then check out external testing.[9]

Add yourself to this internal testing group by clicking the blue plus sign next to Testers (0). Click the checkbox next to your account and click Add.

Note the Invited flag under the STATUS column. Invited testers receive an email from Apple that must be confirmed before they can download your app.

How to Add More Testers

 All internal testers need to first be App Store Connect users with access to your app. Add a new user from the Users and Access tab at the top of App Store Connect. They will then appear in the previous dialog. More information, including some limitations, can be found in the documentation.[10]

Download the App on TestFlight

Go grab your iOS device and open the email from Apple inviting you to the TestFlight beta—it will come from no_reply@email.apple.com. Tap the big View in TestFlight button. If you don't yet have TestFlight installed, follow the link to do so. Then, accept the invitation and download the app to your device. Once downloaded, TestFlight will open to your app's landing page (see the screenshot on the right, shown on page 181).

Testers can use the TestFlight app to leave feedback for you and receive notifications of new builds.

---

8.   https://developer.apple.com/help/app-store-connect/test-a-beta-version/add-internal-testers

9.   https://developer.apple.com/help/app-store-connect/test-a-beta-version/invite-external-testers/

10. https://developer.apple.com/help/app-store-connect/manage-your-team/add-and-edit-users

OK, the moment we've been waiting for...go ahead and launch the app!

Oh, well, that's unfortunate. It looks like our iOS device can't connect to the server running on our Mac. Can you guess why?

In SceneDelegate we set baseURL to localhost. That works fine when running in the simulator—it creates a round trip back to your Mac. But "localhost" on a physical device is the iOS device itself, not the Mac. You need the TestFlight builds to point directly to your Mac, via its IP address. To do this, you need to update baseURL for release builds.

In your terminal, run networksetup -getinfo Wi-Fi and copy the value of your IP address. Here, mine is 192.168.50.139.

```
~ networksetup -getinfo Wi-Fi
DHCP Configuration
IP address: 192.168.50.139
Subnet mask: 255.255.224.0
Router: 192.168.128.1
Client ID:
IPv6: Automatic
IPv6 IP address: none
IPv6 Router: none
Wi-Fi ID: 5c:e9:1e:6b:08:f4
```

You can then use a *compiler directive* to configure a different URL depending on whether the app was run from Xcode or downloaded via TestFlight. By default, running the app via Product → Run puts it in debug mode so you can attach a debugger and step through code. And archiving a build via Product → Archive is set to release mode, where #if DEBUG returns false.

Update SceneDelegate to set a different baseURL depending on whether the app was built in debug mode or not.

ch09_04/ios/App/Delegates/SceneDelegate.swift
```swift
import HotwireNative
import UIKit

#if DEBUG
let baseURL = URL(string: "http://localhost:3000")!
#else
// NOTE: Your IP address will be different.
let baseURL = URL(string: "http://192.168.50.139:3000")!
#endif

class SceneDelegate: UIResponder, UIWindowSceneDelegate {
    // ...
}
```

Pop back into your terminal and stop the Rails server. Then run it again via bin/rails server -b 0.0.0.0. The -b option binds Rails to a specific IP address. Using 0.0.0.0 binds it to *all* IP addresses, not just localhost.

Back in Xcode, archive and upload a new build one more time. When it finishes processing, download it on your iOS device. Don't forget to declare encryption if you didn't update Info.plist!

Finally, launch the app that now correctly hits the server running on your Mac. You've got an app running on a real device—go show your friends!

Production Server

Be aware that your iOS device must be on the same network as your Mac for this to work. But you can use the same technique when you deploy to a real production server: replace your machine's IP address with the full URL of your website. And if you want to get fancy, you could use an Xcode build configuration file[11] to set up your URLs.

With your iOS app deployed to TestFlight, let's move on to Android. To deploy the app to Android with Play Testing, you'll work through these steps:

1. Set up your app in the Google Play Console.
2. Generate a signed app bundle in Android Studio.
3. Distribute the build to testers.

Add an App to the Play Console

For the first step, you'll start by getting your app in Google Play, Android's equivalent of the App Store. To do that, you need a Play Console developer account.

Create a Play Console Developer Account

We'll follow the steps outlined in this Play Console help document.[12] Start by signing up for a Play Console developer account[13] with a Google account. You will need to verify both an email address and phone number and enable 2-step verification.

Then, visit the Play Console[14] and accept the terms and conditions. From there, follow the wizard to pay the one-time $25 fee and choose between an individual or organization account. Note that either option requires you to verify your identity *and* prove that you have a physical Android device. Identity verification is a manual process done by Google and can take a few days. You won't be able to publish apps, even for internal testing, until your account is verified. You're welcome to continue with the rest of the chapter while you wait. You'll be able to work through everything until the last section, Distribute Builds to Testers, on page 190.

---

11. https://nshipster.com/xcconfig/

12. https://support.google.com/googleplay/android-developer/answer/6112435

13. https://play.google.com/apps/publish/signup

14. https://developer.android.com/distribute/googleplay/developer-console.html

Create a New App in the Play Console

Create a new app by visiting the Play Console[15] and clicking Create app.

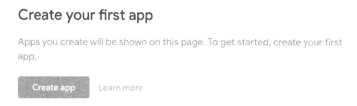

For the app details, enter "Hiking Journal" for App name and select App and Free. Check the boxes to accept the declarations and click Create app.

Create app

App details

App name

Hiking Journal

This is how your app will appear on Google Play   14 / 30

Default language

English (United States) – en-US

App or game   You can change this later in Store settings

⦿ App

◯ Game

Free or paid   You can edit this later on the Paid app page

⦿ Free

◯ Paid

Next, upload the app to Google Play by generating a *signed app bundle* from Android Studio.

Generate and Upload a Signed App Bundle

Before you generate a bundle, let's make sure a physical Android device can access the server running on our Mac. You already learned this lesson when working on your iOS build on page 181—no need to demonstrate it again.

---

15. https://play.google.com/console

Update baseURL for Release Builds

Android uses build variants[16] to represent different versions of your app that you can build. They are configured using a specific set of rules to combine settings, code, and resources configured in your build types. You'll use build variants to set a different baseURL for debug (when run in the emulator) vs. release builds (when signed and uploaded to Google Play).

Start by opening the app's build.gradle.kts and create a second build type, debug, under the buildTypes section.

ch09_05/android/app/build.gradle.kts

```
// ...

android {
    // ...

    buildTypes {
        debug {
        }

        release {
            isMinifyEnabled = false
            proguardFiles(
                getDefaultProguardFile("proguard-android-optimize.txt"),
                "proguard-rules.pro"
            )
        }
    }
    // ...
}
// ...
```

Next, you'll set the BASE_URL build config field for each variant. As a quick refresher, you can get your macOS IP address by running networksetup -getinfo Wi-Fi in your terminal. Here, mine is 192.168.50.139.

```
~ networksetup -getinfo Wi-Fi
DHCP Configuration
IP address: 192.168.50.139
Subnet mask: 255.255.224.0
Router: 192.168.128.1
Client ID:
IPv6: Automatic
IPv6 IP address: none
IPv6 Router: none
Wi-Fi ID: 5c:e9:1e:6b:08:f4
```

---

16. https://developer.android.com/build/build-variants

Add the build config field for both variants, pointing the debug variant to the original IP address and the release variant with your Mac's IP address.

ch09_06/android/app/build.gradle.kts

```
// ...

android {
    // ...

    buildTypes {
        debug {
            buildConfigField(
                type ="String",
                name = "BASE_URL",
                value = "\"http://10.0.2.2:3000\""
            )
        }

        release {
            buildConfigField(
                type ="String",
                name = "BASE_URL",
                // NOTE: Your IP address will be different.
                value = "\"http://192.168.50.139:3000\""
            )
            isMinifyEnabled = false
            proguardFiles(
                getDefaultProguardFile("proguard-android-optimize.txt"),
                "proguard-rules.pro"
            )
        }
    }
    // ...
}
// ...
```

Then, toward the bottom of the file, enable the build config feature in the buildFeatures section.

ch09_07/android/app/build.gradle.kts

```
// ...

android {
    // ...

    buildFeatures {
        compose = true
        buildConfig = true
    }
}
// ...
```

Sync Gradle and rebuild the project via Build → Rebuild project.

Use the new, dynamic URL by opening MainActivity and replacing the value of baseURL with the version from the build config.

ch09_08/android/app/src/main/java/com/masilotti/hikingjournal/activities/MainActivity.kt

```
package com.masilotti.hikingjournal.activities

import android.os.Bundle
import android.view.View
import androidx.activity.enableEdgeToEdge
import com.google.android.material.bottomnavigation.BottomNavigationView
➤ import com.masilotti.hikingjournal.BuildConfig
import com.masilotti.hikingjournal.R
import com.masilotti.hikingjournal.activities.models.mainTabs
import dev.hotwire.navigation.activities.HotwireActivity
import dev.hotwire.navigation.tabs.HotwireBottomNavigationController
import dev.hotwire.navigation.tabs.navigatorConfigurations
import dev.hotwire.navigation.util.applyDefaultImeWindowInsets

➤ const val baseURL = BuildConfig.BASE_URL

class MainActivity : HotwireActivity() {
    // ...
}
```

Next, you'll generate a signed app bundle to upload to Google Play. You'll select the release build variant, which will set the baseURL to our Mac's IP address.

Generate a Signed App Bundle

Select Build → Generate Signed App Bundle / APK... from the Menu Bar. Select Android App Bundle and click Next.

The next screen prompts you for something called a *key store*. An Android key store is a secure storage container that verifies the authenticity of your app. Google Play uses it to verify that updates come from the original developer—you. Apps signed with a key store are also harder to modify and redistribute maliciously.

Generate a new key store by clicking Create new....

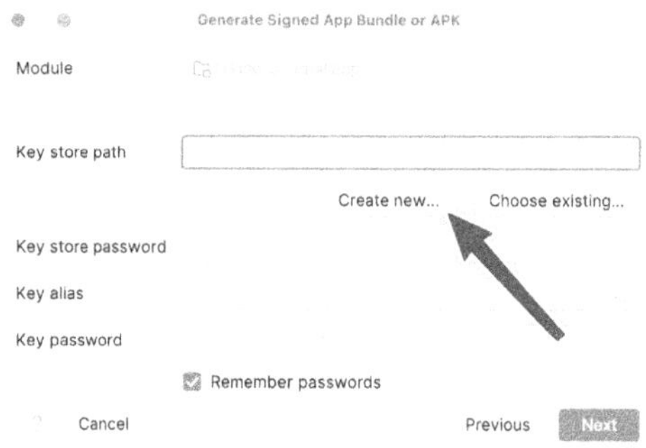

I keep my key store in the same directory as my Android project and add it to .gitignore so it doesn't get checked in with the code. I also use the same password for the key store and the key itself—one less thing to forget. Populate these along with at least one field under the Certificate fieldset. I usually fill in the name because it's first. You can leave the Alias and Validity fields as is. Then click OK.

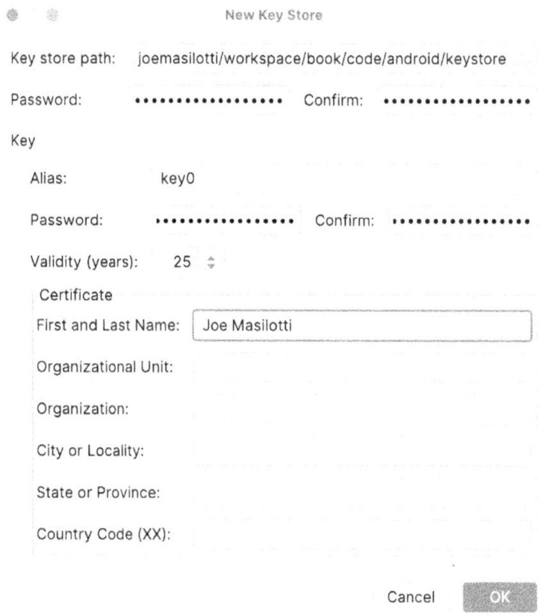

The key store will be selected, and passwords will populate. Make sure "Remember passwords" is checked, and click Next.

	Generate Signed App Bundle or APK
Module	Hiking_Journal.app
Key store path	sers/joemasilotti/workspace/book/code/android/keystore
	Create new... Choose existing...
Key store password	••••••••••••••••••••
Key alias	key0
Key password	••••••••••••••••••••
	☑ Remember passwords
? Cancel	Previous Next

The next screen asks which build variant we want to build the app with. Select "release" to ensure the correct baseURL is used from earlier. Click Create.

	Generate Signed App Bundle or APK
Destination Folder:	/Users/joemasilotti/workspace/book/code/android
	debug
	release
Build Variants:	
? Cancel	Previous Create

When the signed bundle finishes generating, a small dialog will appear in the bottom right of the screen in Android Studio. Click it to expand it, and then click the "locate" link to open the containing folder.

> ℹ **Generate Signed Bundle**   ⋮ ✕
> App bundle(s) generated successfully for
> module 'Hiking_Journal.app.main' with 1 build
> variant:
> Build variant 'release': locate or analyze the
> app bundle.
>   ∧

With your signed bundle in hand, you can upload it to the Play Console.

Upload the Signed Bundle to the Play Console

Sign in to the Play Console[17] and select your app. From the sidebar on the left, navigate to Test and release → Testing → Internal testing. Click "Create new release" in the upper right.

Drag and drop the signed bundle into the App bundles area in the middle of the form. This will take a minute or two to upload and validate. While you wait for that, enter a release name. I used "1 (1.0)" since this is the first build for version 1.0 of the app. When validation completes, click Next in the bottom right.

Manifest Conflicts Error

 If you're seeing the following error message, then you'll need to change your bundle identifier to avoid conflicts with my app. Do this by changing applicationId in the app's build.gradle.kts.

Remove conflicts from the manifest before uploading. The following content provider authorities are in use by other developers: com.masilotti.hikingjournal.androidx-startup, com.masilotti.hikingjournal.com.pairip.licensecheck.LicenseContentProvider, com.masilotti.hikingjournal.hotwire.fileprovider.
You need to use a different package name because "com.masilotti.hikingjournal" already exists in Google Play.

On the next screen, click Save and publish. Note that this button will only be active once Google verifies your developer account.

You can now distribute your published app to testers!

Distribute Builds to Testers

Just like for iOS, you'll create an email list of testers to invite to your app. Google Play has a concept of *tracks*—an app is promoted along these as the

---

17. https://play.google.com/console/

audience grows. The first track is internal testing,[18] which is limited to 100 testers but doesn't require any manual review from Google.

From the Google Play Console, navigate to Test and release → Testing → Internal testing. Select the Testers tab, and then click "Create email list."

Name the list "Internal Testers." Then, add your email to the second field and press ↵. Click the "Save changes" button in the bottom right to create the email list.

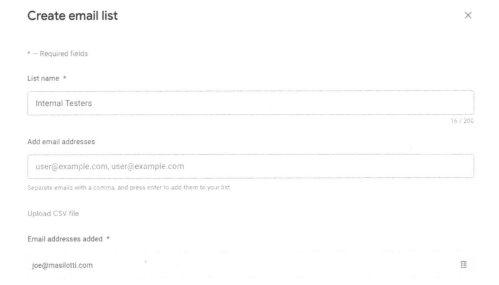

After the list is created, click Save in the bottom right of the Internal testing screen.

Google won't send an invitation like Apple. Instead, you'll send a link to the testers manually. At the bottom of the screen, click "Copy link" to copy the URL to your clipboard, as shown in the screenshot on page 192.

18. https://play.google.com/console/about/internal-testing

Open that URL on your Android device. I pasted mine into an email and signed into the Gmail app on my Android device.

Click Accept Invite at the bottom of the screen, and then click the Google Play download link to install the app on your device.

Once the app is installed, click Open. Congratulations! Your app is now running on your Android device.

You may have noticed that, unlike on iOS, we didn't have to set an app icon for Android. But if you're so inclined, feel free to add one by following this Android Developer codelab.[19]

What's Next?

In this chapter, you learned how to deploy your app to real-world, physical devices with App Store Connect and the Google Play Console. Both platforms

---

19. https://developer.android.com/codelabs/basic-android-kotlin-compose-training-change-app-icon#0

required minor code changes to use a different baseURL when built for distribution. On iOS, we hardcoded an #if DEBUG statement, and on Android we used a build variant for release builds. You also learned how to correctly code sign your apps for Apple and Google to verify that you did indeed build them.

So far, you've only invited yourself to the two releases. Try adding a second or third tester from App Store Connect and the Play Console. Gather feedback on your app from a larger group! Just make sure they are on the same network as your Mac and you keep your server running. Or, deploy the Rails app somewhere online and update baseURL—then your app will be accessible to anyone, anywhere.

Submit to the App Stores

Submitting your apps to the App Store and Google Play is only a few more steps. But there's nothing special needed for Hotwire Native apps. You can follow along with Apple's guide for the App Store[20] and Google's guide for Google Play.[21]

Now that you have the apps registered with Apple and Google, you can start integrating with their services, like push notifications. In the next and final chapter, you'll learn how to configure, register for, and send push notifications when someone likes a hike.

---

20. https://developer.apple.com/ios/submit/

21. https://support.google.com/googleplay/android-developer/answer/9859348?hl=en

## CHAPTER 10

Send Push Notifications with APNs and FCM

One of the biggest selling points of a native mobile app is push notifications. Sometimes, it's *the* reason my clients need an app over a website. This is because push notifications are instant, reliable, and drive higher engagement than email or SMS. And even with recent enhancements to Progressive Web Apps (PWAs), native apps are still the best way to send reliable, timely notifications.

In this chapter, you'll learn how to configure, register, and send a push notification to iOS devices (via Apple Push Notification service (APNs)) and Android devices (via Firebase Cloud Messaging (FCM)). Specifically, whenever a user of your app likes a hike (by tapping the heart on a hike page), you'll use a push notification to let the owner of the hike know. This is what the user will see:

This final chapter combines everything you've learned throughout the book so far. You'll create an authenticated Rails endpoint, build bridge components, and write native code. If you get stuck, just take your time. Or take a quick break. Try not to get discouraged. Remember, you can always double-check your work by looking at the reference code for each checkpoint.

Before we dive into any code, it's important to understand the fundamental infrastructure of push notifications. Luckily, both platforms work in a similar way, so we can talk about them in general terms.

Send Push Notifications from Ruby on Rails

To send a user a push notification, you first need the user's permission to do so. This is triggered by a call to a native API that then presents a system dialog, shown as follows. If the user accepts, the system provides us with a *notification token* unique to the device.

You'll transfer this token to your Rails server and use the Noticed gem[1] to communicate with APNs and FCM. These services will then send the notification to the device, identified by its token. It's important to note that you don't directly send notifications to devices. You request APNs and FCM to do so via HTTP requests (abstracted by the Noticed gem).

Let's start with the Rails code. This section will walk you through the following steps:

1. Create a bridge component to trigger the native system dialog.
2. Create a notification token model and migration to persist tokens.
3. Add a route and controller to receive notification tokens.
4. Add the Noticed gem to send notifications.
5. Authenticate APNs.

---

1. https://github.com/excid3/noticed

Did You Skip the Previous Chapter?

If you skipped Chapter 9, Deploy to Physical Devices with Test-Flight and Play Testing, on page 171, you'll need to register your app with Apple to be able to send iOS notifications via APNs. Work through all of Add an App to App Store Connect, on page 172, to get yours set up.

Create a Bridge Component

The bridge component will tell the apps it's time to ask the user for permission to send notifications. First, generate a new Stimulus controller by running the following in the rails directory:

```
bin/rails generate stimulus bridge/notification_token
```

Replace the import statement and parent class to convert the Stimulus controller to a bridge component.

ch10_01/rails/app/javascript/controllers/bridge/notification_token_controller.js
```
import { BridgeComponent } from "@hotwired/hotwire-native-bridge"

export default class extends BridgeComponent {
}
```

Then, identify the component as "notification-token".

ch10_02/rails/app/javascript/controllers/bridge/notification_token_controller.js
```
import { BridgeComponent } from "@hotwired/hotwire-native-bridge"

export default class extends BridgeComponent {
  static component = "notification-token"
}
```

Wrap up this file by firing the "connect" message via send() when the controller connects.

ch10_03/rails/app/javascript/controllers/bridge/notification_token_controller.js
```
import { BridgeComponent } from "@hotwired/hotwire-native-bridge"

export default class extends BridgeComponent {
  static component = "notification-token"

  connect() {
    super.connect()
    this.send("connect")
  }
}
```

Wire up the controller by adding a data-controller to the hikes index page, wrapped inside of user_signed_in?. By using a bridge component, we can use

Ruby to determine if the user is signed in and avoid any authentication logic in the native apps.

ch10_04/rails/app/views/hikes/index.html.erb
```erb
<%= render "shared/header", title: "Hikes" %>

<% if user_signed_in? %>
  <meta data-controller="bridge--notification-token">
<% end %>

<% if @hikes.any? %>
  <div class="container list-group list-group-flush px-0">
    <%= render @hikes %>
  </div>
<% else %>
  <p class="container">No hikes, yet.</p>
<% end %>

<%# ... %>
```

When the user accepts the triggered system dialog, you'll POST the notification token to your server. You'll come back and implement that code in the iOS and the Android sections later in the chapter. Right now, you're building the core infrastructure needed to receive and persist these tokens to the Rails database.

Create the Notification Token Model

You'll keep track of a user's notification tokens with a new database table and record. We'll then use this to know *where* to send the notifications. Switch to the rails directory and generate the migration and model with the following:

```
bin/rails generate model NotificationToken \
  user:references! token:string! platform:string!
```

This creates a NotificationToken record that belongs to a User. It has a token column, the notification token from the device, and a platform column, to differentiate between iOS and Android devices. The three exclamation points (!) ensure that these columns cannot be null, adding null: false to the migration. Run the migration with bin/rails db:migrate.

Open rails/app/models/notification_token.rb and add the following validations. These ensure we always have a token and, for now, only for iOS devices. We'll add FCM later in the Android section.

ch10_06/rails/app/models/notification_token.rb
```ruby
class NotificationToken < ApplicationRecord
  belongs_to :user

  validates :token, presence: true
  validates :platform, inclusion: {in: %w[iOS]}
end
```

Next, create the inverse association to the NotificationToken on the User model. A user can have more than one token because they can sign into the app on multiple devices and we want to notify each device.

ch10_07/rails/app/models/user.rb

```ruby
class User < ApplicationRecord
  has_secure_password

  has_many :hikes
  has_many :hike_likes
  has_many :liked_hikes, through: :hike_likes, source: :hike
➤ has_many :notification_tokens

  validates :name, presence: true
  validates :email, presence: true, uniqueness: true

  normalizes :email, with: -> { _1.strip.downcase }
end
```

To get the token into the database, we need an endpoint for the apps to POST to. Up next, we'll create a new route and controller to register the notification token.

Add a Route and Controller

Add a new entry to routes.rb to create a new route for creating notification tokens.

ch10_08/rails/config/routes.rb

```ruby
Rails.application.routes.draw do
  resource :session, only: %i[new create destroy]

  resources :hikes do
    resource :map, only: :show
    resources :likes, only: %w[create destroy]
  end

  resources :users, only: :index do
    resources :hikes, only: :index, controller: :user_hikes
  end

➤ resources :notification_tokens, only: :create

  resources :configurations, only: [] do
    get :ios_v1, on: :collection
    get :android_v1, on: :collection
  end

  root "hikes#index"
end
```

Then, create a new controller and name it NotificationTokensController. Add an empty #create method.

ch10_09/rails/app/controllers/notification_tokens_controller.rb
```
class NotificationTokensController < ApplicationController
  def create
  end
end
```

Inside the #create method, find or create a notification token for the current user. #find_or_create_by!() will use the given parameters to first check if a matching record exists. If none exists, a new record is created. The exclamation point (!) will cause any failure to raise an exception.

ch10_10/rails/app/controllers/notification_tokens_controller.rb
```
class NotificationTokensController < ApplicationController
  def create
    current_user.notification_tokens.find_or_create_by!(notification_token)
  end

  private

  def notification_token
    params.require(:notification_token).permit(:token, :platform)
  end
end
```

To use current_user, authenticate the user in a before_action at the top of the file. In the native apps, we'll copy over the authenticated cookie from the web view to the incoming HTTP request, allowing us to reuse the existing logic from the Authentication concern. The request will be JSON, so it won't include the cross-site request forgery (CSRF)[2] token to validate the request. So make sure to disable CSRF protection by skipping the verify_authenticity_token action.

ch10_11/rails/app/controllers/notification_tokens_controller.rb
```
class NotificationTokensController < ApplicationController
  before_action :authenticate_user!

  skip_before_action :verify_authenticity_token

  def create
    current_user.notification_tokens.find_or_create_by!(notification_token)
  end

  private

  def notification_token
    params.require(:notification_token).permit(:token, :platform)
  end
end
```

---

2. https://guides.rubyonrails.org/security.html#cross-site-request-forgery-csrf

This is another example of how you're keeping your logic on the server. Traditional mobile apps would need their own authentication token or even a JWT to authorize network requests. Instead, you're reusing the existing web cookie across web and native. That simplifies your logic immensely—you only have one authentication strategy to manage. If the cookie ever expires or becomes invalidated, *both* web and native requests will correctly fail.

Wrap up this file by responding with a 201 status code, "Created," to let the apps know the record was created successfully.

ch10_12/rails/app/controllers/notification_tokens_controller.rb

```ruby
class NotificationTokensController < ApplicationController
  before_action :authenticate_user!

  skip_before_action :verify_authenticity_token

  def create
    current_user.notification_tokens.find_or_create_by!(notification_token)
    head :created
  end

  private

  def notification_token
    params.require(:notification_token).permit(:token, :platform)
  end
end
```

Devices can now POST to /notification_tokens to register their tokens with the Rails server. Up next, let's learn how to send a notification when someone likes a hike.

Send Push Notifications with Noticed

To send a notification to an iOS device, you need to send an authenticated HTTP request to Apple Push Notification service (APNs). Instead of doing this manually, I like to use the Noticed gem[3] to abstract away the annoying parts. Noticed will also help keep your code organized with a Notifier subclass—here, you could configure different types of notifications like SMS, Email, Discord, and more.

Start by adding the Noticed and Apnotic[4] gems by switching to the rails directory and executing bundle add noticed apnotic. Noticed uses Apnotic under the hood to authorize and manage network connections to APNs.

---

3.   https://github.com/excid3/noticed
4.   https://github.com/ostinelli/apnotic

Install the Noticed migrations by running `bin/rails noticed:install:migrations` and migrating the database with `bin/rails db:migrate`.

Notifications are sent via `Notifier` subclasses from Noticed. Create a new one by running `bin/rails generate noticed:notifier NewLikeNotifier`. This will create `NewLikeNotifier` and `ApplicationNotifier` under `app/notifiers`. Use `ApplicationNotifier` to store generic or reusable logic for your notifiers, like `ApplicationController` does for your controllers.

In `NewLikeNotifier`, replace the `deliver_by` with one for iOS. Each `deliver_by` block can configure a different type of notification platform like ActionCable, Email, SMS, and more.[5]

ch10_15/rails/app/notifiers/new_like_notifier.rb
```ruby
class NewLikeNotifier < ApplicationNotifier
  deliver_by :ios do |config|
  end
end
```

Gather each recipient's notification tokens via `config.device_tokens`, making sure to scope the query to only the iOS platform.

ch10_16/rails/app/notifiers/new_like_notifier.rb
```ruby
class NewLikeNotifier < ApplicationNotifier
  deliver_by :ios do |config|
    config.device_tokens = -> {
      recipient.notification_tokens.where(platform: :iOS).pluck(:token)
    }
  end
end
```

Then, configure what the user sees when a notification appears on their device via `config.format`.

ch10_17/rails/app/notifiers/new_like_notifier.rb
```ruby
class NewLikeNotifier < ApplicationNotifier
  deliver_by :ios do |config|
    config.device_tokens = -> {
      recipient.notification_tokens.where(platform: :iOS).pluck(:token)
    }

    config.format = ->(apn) {
      apn.alert = "Someone liked your hike!"
    }
  end
end
```

---

5. https://github.com/excid3/noticed?tab=readme-ov-file#-delivery-methods

Here, you're setting alert to display a message to the user to let them know someone liked their hike. Check out the Apnotic documentation[6] for all the options you can use for notifications.

One of those options is custom_payload. This is a special option reserved for application-specific, custom logic. Use this to include the path of the hike. When the user opens the notification, you can use this option to build a URL and deep link to the hike's page.

```
ch10_18/rails/app/notifiers/new_like_notifier.rb
class NewLikeNotifier < ApplicationNotifier
  required_param :hike

  deliver_by :ios do |config|
    config.device_tokens = -> {
      recipient.notification_tokens.where(platform: :iOS).pluck(:token)
    }

    config.format = ->(apn) {
      apn.alert = "Someone liked your hike!"
      apn.custom_payload = {
        path: hike_path(params[:hike])
      }
    }
  end
end
```

required_param :hike forces us to pass in an object with the hike: keyword when creating the notification, like so: NewLikeNotifier.with(hike: Hike.first).

Along with the device token, you need to authenticate your Apple Developer account with APNs. Configure the four required attributes, reading each from Rails credentials. We'll come back and add these to your development credentials later.

```
ch10_19/rails/app/notifiers/new_like_notifier.rb
class NewLikeNotifier < ApplicationNotifier
  required_param :hike

  deliver_by :ios do |config|
    # ...
    config.format = ->(apn) {
      # ...
    }

    credentials = Rails.application.credentials.ios
    config.bundle_identifier = credentials.bundle_identifier
    config.key_id = credentials.key_id
    config.team_id = credentials.team_id
```

---

6. https://github.com/ostinelli/apnotic#apnoticnotification

```
    config.apns_key = credentials.apns_key
  end
end
```

Wrap up this file by setting the development, or sandbox, environment flag. This allows you to send notifications to apps built in debug mode, such as when running from Xcode on the simulator. When you deploy to a staging or production server, Rails.env.local? will return false, setting the APNs environment to production.

ch10_20/rails/app/notifiers/new_like_notifier.rb
```
class NewLikeNotifier < ApplicationNotifier
  required_param :hike

  deliver_by :ios do |config|
    # ...

    credentials = Rails.application.credentials.ios
    config.bundle_identifier = credentials.bundle_identifier
    config.key_id = credentials.key_id
    config.team_id = credentials.team_id
    config.apns_key = credentials.apns_key

    config.development = Rails.env.local?
  end
end
```

Wrap up your Rails code changes by triggering the notification in likes_controller.rb when a new Like is created.

ch10_21/rails/app/controllers/likes_controller.rb
```
class LikesController < ApplicationController
  before_action :authenticate_user!

  def create
    hike = Hike.find(params[:hike_id])
    hike.likes.find_or_create_by!(user: current_user)
    NewLikeNotifier.with(hike: hike).deliver(hike.user)
    redirect_to hike
  end

  def destroy
    # ...
  end
end
```

Alright, all that's left is populating those credentials. Let's do that now.

Authenticate APNs

Wrap up the server code by authenticating the requests to APNs.

Sign in to your Apple Developer account[7] and click Keys from the Certificates, IDs & Profiles column in the middle.

Then, click the blue plus button at the top or Create a key. Enter a descriptive name for the name of the key and check the box next to Apple Push Notifications service (APNs). Click Continue. On the next screen, click Register.

Register a New Key

Key Name

Hiking Journal APNs key

You cannot use special characters such as @, &, ', ", .,

Key Usage Description (optional)

ENABLE	NAME	DESCRIPTION
☑	Apple Push Notifications service (APNs)	Establish connectivity between your notification server and the Apple Push Notification service. One key is used for all of your apps. Learn more

When the key generates, click Download to save a copy to your machine. Note that you won't be able to download this again after navigating away from the page. Store it somewhere safe!

Enable push notifications for your App Identifier by clicking Identifiers on the left and then selecting your identifier from the list. Scroll down and check the box next to Push Notifications and then click Save.

Certificates, Identifiers & Profiles

‹ All Identifiers

Edit your App ID Configuration   Remove   Save

Platform   App ID Prefix
IOS, iPadOS, macOS, tvOS, watchOS, visionOS   6J82VP4ATY (Team ID)

Description   Bundle ID
Hiking Journal app identifier   com.masilotti.HikingJournal (explicit)

You cannot use special characters such as @, &, ', "

Capabilities   App Services

ENABLE	NAME		NOTES
☑	Push Notifications Broadcast Capability	Configure	Certificates (0)

Back in your terminal, edit your development credentials by running the following command from the rails directory:

```
bin/rails credentials:edit --environment development
```

Add a top-level ios: key with four fields to reflect what we added to NewLikeNotifier:

- bundle_identifier—com.masilotti.HikingJournal, updated to your bundle identifier
- key_id—found on the confirmation page when the key is created

---

7. https://developer.apple.com/account

- team_id—all the way in the upper right on the same page
- apns_key—the downloaded .p8 file as plain-text

For the last field, use |- to collapse white space for a multiline string. This allows you to copy-paste the private key without worrying about formatting. Here's what my decrypted credentials file looks like for an old key:

```
ios:
  bundle_identifier: com.masilotti.HikingJournal
  key_id: C3P98234KT
  team_id: 6JS2VP4ATY
  apns_key: |-
    -----BEGIN PRIVATE KEY-----
    MIGTAgEAMBMGByqGSM49AgEGCCqGSM49AwEHBHkwdwIBAQQgZx5PD8rL5JqwMcKt
    pT9SXTkFmNlJ3oWmTG3DRKv5H2OgCgYIKoZIzj0DAQehRANCAAQw1eXZF7L+tx0h
    pKZy9fEdqYtBPsUq4kYHTgYKMfHv7NpytC0JXMGt29zDbHSiZnHtqiwvGTxE/WEj
    yVRgKXrs
    -----END PRIVATE KEY-----
```

Your Rails server is now set up to send push notifications to iOS devices. It can trigger the authorization dialog with the bridge component, persist the NotificationToken records to the database, and send notifications with NewLikeNotifier. Up next, we'll tackle the native iOS code before moving on to Android.

Configure iOS for Push Notifications

To configure iOS for push notifications, our path will mirror what we did in Rails:

1. Create a bridge component to authorize the sending of notifications.
2. POST the token to /notification_tokens from a view model.
3. Pass the token from AppDelegate to the view model.
4. Configure entitlements for push notifications.
5. Route, or deep-link, notifications.

Create an iOS Bridge Component

Start by creating a new bridge component under the Components folder named NotificationTokenComponent. Identify this the same as the one on the web, "notification-token."

ch10_22/ios/App/Components/NotificationTokenComponent.swift
```swift
import HotwireNative
import UIKit

class NotificationTokenComponent: BridgeComponent {
    override class var name: String { "notification-token" }
}
```

Just as in Chapter 7, Build iOS Bridge Components with Swift, on page 127, you'll use onReceive(message:) to handle incoming messages.

Add this and call a new private function to request notification permissions.

```
ch10_23/ios/App/Components/NotificationTokenComponent.swift
import HotwireNative
import UIKit

class NotificationTokenComponent: BridgeComponent {
    override class var name: String { "notification-token" }

➤   override func onReceive(message: Message) {
➤       Task { await requestNotificationPermission() }
➤   }
➤
➤   private func requestNotificationPermission() async {
➤   }
}
```

The upcoming code to authorize notifications is an asynchronous operation, hence the async keyword on requestNotificationPermission(). Combined with Task { await ... }, we can pop off of the current thread and perform the task. We used a similar technique in MapView when we called viewModel.fetchCoordinates().

Inside of the new function, request notification authorization for the following three options: alerts, sounds, and badges. If the user accepts, register for notifications via the shared UIApplication instance.

```
ch10_24/ios/App/Components/NotificationTokenComponent.swift
import HotwireNative
import UIKit

class NotificationTokenComponent: BridgeComponent {
    override class var name: String { "notification-token" }

    override func onReceive(message: Message) {
        Task { await requestNotificationPermission() }
    }

    private func requestNotificationPermission() async {
➤       let center = UNUserNotificationCenter.current()
➤       let options: UNAuthorizationOptions = [.alert, .sound, .badge]
➤       if try await center.requestAuthorization(options: options) {
➤           UIApplication.shared.registerForRemoteNotifications()
➤       }
    }
}
```

These three options are the most common combination when sending a notification on iOS. Check out the documentation[8] for the full list of notification options.

To address the compilation error, wrap the entire body of the function in a do/catch block, printing any runtime errors that occur.

ch10_25/ios/App/Components/NotificationTokenComponent.swift
```
import HotwireNative
import UIKit

class NotificationTokenComponent: BridgeComponent {
    override class var name: String { "notification-token" }

    override func onReceive(message: Message) {
        Task { await requestNotificationPermission() }
    }

    private func requestNotificationPermission() async {
        do {
            let center = UNUserNotificationCenter.current()
            let options: UNAuthorizationOptions = [.alert, .sound, .badge]
            if try await center.requestAuthorization(options: options) {
                UIApplication.shared.registerForRemoteNotifications()
            }
        } catch {
            print("Failed to authorize: \(error.localizedDescription)")
        }
    }
}
```

That's all for the bridge component. Now, when data--bridge--notification-token appears in the HTML, the user will be prompted to receive push notifications.

Make sure Hotwire Native is aware of the component by registering it in AppDelegate.

ch10_26/ios/App/Delegates/AppDelegate.swift
```
import HotwireNative
import UIKit

@main
class AppDelegate: UIResponder, UIApplicationDelegate {
    func application(
        _ application: UIApplication,
        didFinishLaunchingWithOptions launchOptions:
        [UIApplication.LaunchOptionsKey: Any]?
    ) -> Bool {
        Hotwire.loadPathConfiguration(from: [
```

8. https://developer.apple.com/documentation/usernotifications/unauthorizationoptions

```
            .server(baseURL.appending(path: "configurations/ios_v1.json"))
        ])

        Hotwire.registerBridgeComponents([
            ButtonComponent.self,
            NotificationTokenComponent.self
        ])

        return true
    }
}
```

iOS informs developers when a token is available by calling a special function. Implement that in AppDelegate like so:

ch10_27/ios/App/Delegates/AppDelegate.swift
```
import HotwireNative
import UIKit

@main
class AppDelegate: UIResponder, UIApplicationDelegate {
    func application(
        _ application: UIApplication,
        didFinishLaunchingWithOptions launchOptions:
        [UIApplication.LaunchOptionsKey: Any]?
    ) -> Bool {
        // ...
    }

    func application(
        _ application: UIApplication,
        didRegisterForRemoteNotificationsWithDeviceToken deviceToken: Data
    ) {
        // POST token to server.
    }
}
```

While we're here, also add the function when registering that a token fails.

ch10_28/ios/App/Delegates/AppDelegate.swift
```
import HotwireNative
import UIKit

@main
class AppDelegate: UIResponder, UIApplicationDelegate {
    func application(
        _ application: UIApplication,
        didFinishLaunchingWithOptions launchOptions:
        [UIApplication.LaunchOptionsKey: Any]?
    ) -> Bool {
        // ...
    }

    func application(
```

```
        _ application: UIApplication,
        didRegisterForRemoteNotificationsWithDeviceToken deviceToken: Data
    ) {
        // POST token to server.
    }

    func application(
        _ application: UIApplication,
        didFailToRegisterForRemoteNotificationsWithError error: any Error
    ) {
        print("Failed to register token: \(error.localizedDescription)")
    }
}
```

To get the deviceToken off of the device and onto your server, you need to make an HTTP request. Following the pattern we used in HikeViewModel from Create a View Model, on page 94, you'll create another view model to do the same.

POST the iOS Token from a View Model

Create a new file under ViewModels and name it NotificationTokenViewModel. Add an empty async function to register a token.

ch10_29/ios/App/ViewModels/NotificationTokenViewModel.swift
```
import Foundation

class NotificationTokenViewModel {
    func register(_ token: String) async {
    }
}
```

Next, build a URLRequest pointing to the /notification_tokens route you created on the server earlier. Set the HTTP method to POST and the required headers for the Rails app to parse the incoming payload as JSON.

ch10_30/ios/App/ViewModels/NotificationTokenViewModel.swift
```
import Foundation

class NotificationTokenViewModel {
    func register(_ token: String) async {
        let url = baseURL.appending(path: "notification_tokens")

        var req = URLRequest(url: url)
        req.httpMethod = "POST"
        req.setValue("application/json", forHTTPHeaderField: "Accept")
        req.setValue("application/json", forHTTPHeaderField: "Content-Type")
    }
}
```

We'll encode the notification token in an Encodable, similar to what we did for Hike in HikeViewModel.

Create a new file under Models and name it NotificationToken.swift. Inside, create a struct that holds a token and a platform. The platform matches the validation we added to the notification_token.rb record on the server.

```
ch10_31/ios/App/Models/NotificationToken.swift
struct NotificationToken: Encodable {
    let token: String
    let platform = "iOS"
}
```

Back in NotificationTokenViewModel, create a NotificationToken, encode it, and add it to the body of the request. Then, initiate the network request via the shared URLSession.

```
ch10_32/ios/App/ViewModels/NotificationTokenViewModel.swift
import Foundation

class NotificationTokenViewModel {
    func register(_ token: String) async {
        let url = baseURL.appending(path: "notification_tokens")

        var req = URLRequest(url: url)
        req.httpMethod = "POST"
        req.setValue("application/json", forHTTPHeaderField: "Accept")
        req.setValue("application/json", forHTTPHeaderField: "Content-Type")

➤       let body = NotificationToken(token: token)
➤       req.httpBody = try JSONEncoder().encode(body)
➤
➤       _ = try await URLSession.shared.data(for: req)
    }
}
```

Finish this file by addressing the compilation error—wrap the new code in a do/catch block and log the error.

```
ch10_33/ios/App/ViewModels/NotificationTokenViewModel.swift
import Foundation

class NotificationTokenViewModel {
    func register(_ token: String) async {
        let url = baseURL.appending(path: "notification_tokens")

        var req = URLRequest(url: url)
        req.httpMethod = "POST"
        req.setValue("application/json", forHTTPHeaderField: "Accept")
        req.setValue("application/json", forHTTPHeaderField: "Content-Type")

➤       do {
            let body = NotificationToken(token: token)
```

```
            req.httpBody = try JSONEncoder().encode(body)

            _ = try await URLSession.shared.data(for: req)
➤      } catch {
➤          print("Failed to POST token: \(error.localizedDescription)")
➤      }
    }
}
```

Where's the Cookie?

On the Rails endpoint, we're using current_user to authenticate the user via a cookie. But we didn't do anything with cookies in the native HTTP request on iOS. So, where does it come from?

Hotwire Native iOS takes care of this for us automatically. After every web request completes successfully, each cookie is copied over from the web view to the cookie jar used for native HTTP requests.

Here's what that code looks like from Hotwire Native iOS:

```
// hotwire-native-ios:Source/Turbo/Navigator/Navigator.swift

extension Navigator: SessionDelegate {
    public func sessionDidFinishRequest(_ session: Session) {
        guard let url = session.activeVisitable?.visitableURL
        else { return }

        let store = WKWebsiteDataStore.default().httpCookieStore
        store.getAllCookies { cookies in
            HTTPCookieStorage.shared.setCookies(
                cookies,
                for: url,
                mainDocumentURL: url
            )
        }
    }
}
```

The view model can now send a String token to the server. We only need a way to get the token to register(_:). Remember that function we left empty in AppDelegate? We'll address that next.

Pass the Token from AppDelegate

Open AppDelegate and create a private instance property for the view model. Then, from the empty function, pass deviceToken to the view model. Don't forget to wrap the call with Task { await ... } since the view model function, register(_:), is marked with async.

ch10_34/ios/App/Delegates/AppDelegate.swift

```swift
// ...

@main
class AppDelegate: UIResponder, UIApplicationDelegate {
    private let viewModel = NotificationTokenViewModel()

    func application(
        _ application: UIApplication,
        didFinishLaunchingWithOptions launchOptions:
        [UIApplication.LaunchOptionsKey: Any]?
    ) -> Bool {
        // ...
    }

    func application(
        _ application: UIApplication,
        didRegisterForRemoteNotificationsWithDeviceToken deviceToken: Data
    ) {
        Task { await viewModel.register(deviceToken) }
    }
    // ...
}
```

Unfortunately, Xcode isn't happy. deviceToken is coming in as Data, but our
function accepts a String:

> Cannot convert value of type 'Data' to expected argument type 'String'

Device tokens come from APNs as binary data for performance reasons.[9] To
convert it to a String, we can map over each character, format it, and then join
everything back to a single string.

ch10_35/ios/App/Delegates/AppDelegate.swift

```swift
// ...

@main
class AppDelegate: UIResponder, UIApplicationDelegate {
    // ...

    func application(
        _ application: UIApplication,
        didRegisterForRemoteNotificationsWithDeviceToken deviceToken: Data
    ) {
        let token = deviceToken.map { String(format: "%02x", $0) }.joined()
        Task { await viewModel.register(token) }
    }
    // ...
}
```

---

9. https://developer.apple.com/documentation/appkit/nsapplicationdelegate/application(_:didregisterforremoteno-
    tificationswithdevicetoken:)

With that, we have all the Swift code we need to register notification tokens with our Rails server. Go ahead and run the app. When you sign in, you should see the system prompt requesting permission to send push notifications.

But, when you tap Allow, you won't see the expected network request hitting the server. Check out the message in the Debug Area at the bottom of the screen. (You can toggle it with View → Debug Area → Show Debug Area.)

We need to enable the Push Notification capability for our app before APNs will provide a notification token.

Configure Entitlements for Push Notifications

Click the HikingJournal project from the Project Navigator on the left, select HikingJournal from the TARGETS (not PROJECT) in the middle column, then select the Signing & Capabilities tab at the top.

Click the Add Capability button in the middle of the screen, titled "+ Capability".

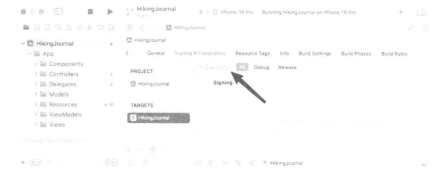

In the dialog that appears, start typing "push" to filter the list and double-click Push Notifications when it appears.

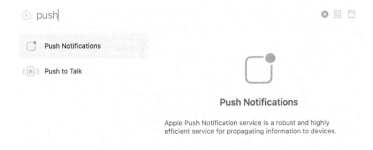

Adding this capability will add a new entitlements file to the Xcode project. Personally, I don't like it floating at the root level. Drag and drop it into the Resources folder. The full name of this file is HikingJournal.entitlements, but Xcode will hide the extension.

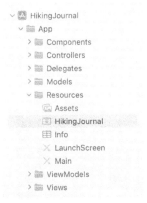

As we did for Info.plist in Clean Up the iOS Directories, on page 62, we need to tell Xcode the new location of the file. Open the target's Build Settings and search for "entitlements" in the upper right. Then, update the value for Code Signing Entitlements to point to the new path: App/Resources/HikingJournal.entitlements, as shown in the screenshot on page 216.

Run the app and watch your server logs. You should see a POST request hit /notification_tokens after signing in. To verify, open a Rails console and inspect the NotificationToken records.

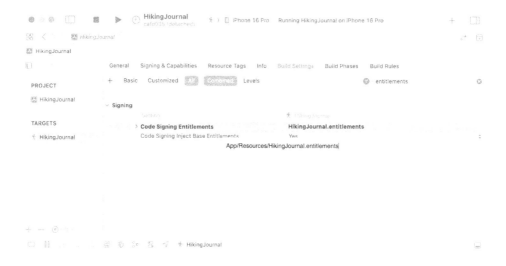

Let's test the entire flow. First, run the app from Xcode and sign in. Then, in the *Simulator* app (not Xcode), select the Device → Lock menu item. In your machine's browser, navigate to the Forest Park hike and click the heart next to the like count—watch as the iOS app receives a push notification in the simulator!

Open the notification by clicking it in the simulator. The app will open to the home screen. Not very helpful, is it? Up next, you'll open the screen encoded in the `path` parameter of the notification.

Route iOS Notifications

This final section for iOS takes your push notifications to another level. When the user taps on a notification, the page of the liked hike will appear on the navigation stack.

Start by creating a new file under Models named NotificationRouter.swift. Create a class that inherits from NSObject and implements the UNUserNotificationCenterDelegate protocol.

ch10_37/ios/App/Models/NotificationRouter.swift
```
import HotwireNative
import UserNotifications

class NotificationRouter: NSObject, UNUserNotificationCenterDelegate {
}
```

The UNUserNotificationCenterDelegate protocol provides a few hooks for us to configure how notifications are received and displayed. Check out the documentation[10] for some use cases.

When a notification is received, userNotificationCenter(_:didReceive:) is called. Declare this function now.

ch10_39/ios/App/Models/NotificationRouter.swift
```
import HotwireNative
import UserNotifications

class NotificationRouter: NSObject, UNUserNotificationCenterDelegate {
    @MainActor
    func userNotificationCenter(
        _ center: UNUserNotificationCenter,
        didReceive response: UNNotificationResponse
    ) async {
    }
}
```

To deep link the user to the relevant hike, you need to know what URL to load. You're already including the hike's URL path in each notification—in NewLikeNotifier you set it via custom_payload. You can retrieve this information by digging into the UNNotificationResponse parameter and pulling out userInfo. It's an untyped dictionary, so you have to cast the values before using them.

ch10_40/ios/App/Models/NotificationRouter.swift
```
import HotwireNative
import UserNotifications

class NotificationRouter: NSObject, UNUserNotificationCenterDelegate {
    @MainActor
```

---

10. https://developer.apple.com/documentation/usernotifications/unusernotificationcenterdelegate

```
    func userNotificationCenter(
        _ center: UNUserNotificationCenter,
        didReceive response: UNNotificationResponse
    ) async {
➤       let userInfo = response.notification.request.content.userInfo
➤       if let path = userInfo["path"] as? String {
➤           let url = baseURL.appending(path: path)
➤       }
    }
}
```

But now that you have a URL, how do you get it back to a Navigator?

Enter NavigationHandler. Hotwire Native provides this protocol for exactly this reason—to get back to the Hotwire world from native code.

```
// hotwire-native-ios:Source/NavigationHandler.swift

import Foundation

/// A protocol to bridge back to Hotwire world from a native context. Use
/// this to trigger a new page visit including routing and presentation.
///
/// When responding to `NavigatorDelegate.handle(proposal:navigator:)`, to
/// route a native view controller, pass in an instance of `Navigator` typed
/// as this protocol with a weak reference. This ensures you avoid a
/// circular dependency between the two.
///
/// - Note: See `NumbersViewController` in the demo app for an example.
public protocol NavigationHandler: AnyObject {
    func route(_ url: URL)

    func route(_ proposal: VisitProposal)
}

extension Navigator: NavigationHandler {
    public func route(_ url: URL) {
        route(url, options: VisitOptions(action: .advance), parameters: nil)
    }
}
```

Initializing NotificationRouter with a reference to a NavigationHandler means you can pass along the notification's URL to have it visited with a new screen.

```
ch10_41/ios/App/Models/NotificationRouter.swift
import HotwireNative
import UserNotifications

class NotificationRouter: NSObject, UNUserNotificationCenterDelegate {
➤   private unowned let navigationHandler: NavigationHandler

➤   init(navigationHandler: NavigationHandler) {
➤       self.navigationHandler = navigationHandler
➤   }
```

```
@MainActor
func userNotificationCenter(
    _ center: UNUserNotificationCenter,
    didReceive response: UNNotificationResponse
) async {
    let userInfo = response.notification.request.content.userInfo
    if let path = userInfo["path"] as? String {
        let url = baseURL.appending(path: path)
        navigationHandler.route(url)
    }
}
}
```

Next, we need something to conform to the NavigationHandler protocol. Turns out that those Hotwire Native framework maintainers are pretty smart—HotwireTabBarController already does exactly that! So we can use it directly.

```
// hotwire-native-ios:Source/Turbo/ViewControllers/HotwireTabBarController.swift

import UIKit

/// A tab bar controller that manages multiple tabs, each associated with
/// its own `Navigator` instance.
///
/// This controller loads tabs defined by `HotwireTab` and configures each
/// one with its own `Navigator`. The currently selected tab's navigator
/// is exposed via the `activeNavigator` property.
open class HotwireTabBarController: UITabBarController, NavigationHandler {
    // ...
}
```

Open SceneDelegate and create a private NotificationRouter, passing in the HotwireTabBarController as the navigationHandler parameter. Then, assign the global notification delegate to the NotificationRouter instance. This tells iOS that you want to handle incoming notifications with your custom router.

```
ch10_43/ios/App/Delegates/SceneDelegate.swift
// ...

class SceneDelegate: UIResponder, UIWindowSceneDelegate {
    var window: UIWindow?

    private lazy var tabBarController = HotwireTabBarController(
        navigatorDelegate: self
    )
    private lazy var notificationRouter = NotificationRouter(
        navigationHandler: tabBarController
    )

    func scene(
        _ scene: UIScene,
```

```
        willConnectTo session: UISceneSession,
        options connectionOptions: UIScene.ConnectionOptions
    ) {
        UNUserNotificationCenter.current().delegate = notificationRouter
        window?.rootViewController = tabBarController
        tabBarController.load(HotwireTab.all)
    }
}
// ...
```

This technique of passing around a NavigationHandler reference is quite useful when building Hotwire Native apps. For example, when rendering a fully native screen, you can call navigationHandler.route(someURL) from a button tap—bridging the gap back to the Hotwire world to present a web-rendered screen.

Test the new and improved notification handling by running the app and locking the simulator again. Trigger a notification by unliking and then liking the Forest Park hike again. When the notification appears, tap it. A new screen gets pushed on the stack, showing the hike!

That's a wrap for push notifications on iOS. Up next, we'll add push notifications to the Android app.

If you're only developing for iOS, then skip ahead to What's Next?, on page 238, to recap everything you've learned and think about how you can apply these lessons further out in the world.

Configure Android for Push Notifications

We'll use Firebase Cloud Messaging[11] (FCM) to send notifications to Android devices.

To configure Android for push notifications, our path will mirror what we did previously:

1. Send FCM notifications from the Rails server.
2. Authenticate our server with FCM.
3. Add FCM dependencies to the Android app.
4. Authorize sending notifications.
5. POST Firebase token to /notification_tokens.
6. Route the notification.

Send FCM Notifications

We'll start by updating our Rails code with a new gem to interact with FCM. Then, we'll add a new deliver_by method to NewLikeNotifier.

Under the hood, Noticed uses the Google Auth Library for Ruby[12] gem to send notifications via FCM. Add this gem by switching to the rails directory and running bundle add googleauth.

Then, add a new option for FCM to the platform validation in NotificationToken. We'll identify notification tokens coming from the Android apps with this value.

ch10_46/rails/app/models/notification_token.rb
```ruby
class NotificationToken < ApplicationRecord
  belongs_to :user

  validates :token, presence: true
  validates :platform, inclusion: {in: %w[iOS FCM]}
end
```

Open NewLikeNotifier and add a new deliver_by method for FCM. Whenever we send a notification, the notifier will run each of the delivery methods.

ch10_47/rails/app/notifiers/new_like_notifier.rb
```ruby
class NewLikeNotifier < ApplicationNotifier
  required_param :hike

  deliver_by :ios do |config|
    # ...
  end
```

---

11. https://firebase.google.com/products/cloud-messaging
12. https://github.com/googleapis/google-auth-library-ruby

```
➤    deliver_by :fcm do |config|
➤      end
    end
```

To make sure we only send notifications to folks who have an FCM token, gather the tokens of the recipient.

ch10_48/rails/app/notifiers/new_like_notifier.rb
```
class NewLikeNotifier < ApplicationNotifier
  # ...

  deliver_by :fcm do |config|
➤    config.device_tokens = -> {
➤      recipient.notification_tokens.where(platform: :FCM).pluck(:token)
➤    }
  end
end
```

Next, format the payload of the notification via config.json. This should look pretty similar to what we did for APNs notifications earlier (especially the path option to deep link to later).

ch10_49/rails/app/notifiers/new_like_notifier.rb
```
class NewLikeNotifier < ApplicationNotifier
  # ...

  deliver_by :fcm do |config|
    config.device_tokens = -> {
      recipient.notification_tokens.where(platform: :FCM).pluck(:token)
    }

➤    config.json = ->(device_token) {
➤      {
➤        message: {
➤          token: device_token,
➤          notification: {
➤            title: "Someone liked your hike!"
➤          },
➤          data: {
➤            path: hike_path(params[:hike])
➤          }
➤        }
➤      }
➤    }
  end
end
```

Wrap up this file by configuring the credentials. Don't forget to call #to_h to convert this to a hash!

```
ch10_50/rails/app/notifiers/new_like_notifier.rb
class NewLikeNotifier < ApplicationNotifier
  # ...

  deliver_by :fcm do |config|
    config.credentials = Rails.application.credentials.fcm.to_h

    config.device_tokens = -> {
      recipient.notification_tokens.where(platform: :FCM).pluck(:token)
    }

    config.json = ->(device_token) {
      # ...
    }
  end
end
```

Our notifier is now set up to send FCM notifications to Android devices. We only need the credentials.

Authenticate FCM

FCM notifications require a (free) Firebase project. Visit the Firebase Console[13] and sign in with a Google account. Then, click Create a project.

Enter Hiking Journal for the project name and click Continue.

Firebase projects can cover multiple platforms, not only Android apps. We'll create an associated Android app next.

When the project page opens, click the gear icon next to Project Overview and select the Project settings option, as shown in the screenshot on page 224.

---

13. https://console.firebase.google.com/

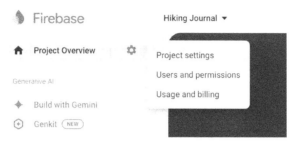

Scroll down and click the Android icon to create a new Android app.

Register the app with a bundle identifier. I'm using com.masilotti.hikingjournal—make sure to change yours to reflect your app. Then click Register app.

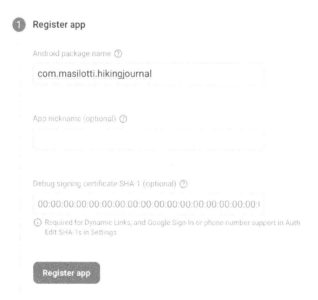

On the next screen, click Next—we'll download this file later when we configure the Android app. Click Continue to Console.

We'll authorize our Rails app with a Firebase service account key. At the top of the Project settings screen, select the Service accounts tab. Then, click

"Generate new private key". Don't worry about which language is selected, that only applies to the code snippet (which we won't use).

Copy the contents of this JSON file to your Rails credentials under the fcm key. Remember, to edit your credentials for the development environment, run the following from the rails directory: bin/rails credentials:edit --environment development.

As you copy this over, make sure to wrap the values for private_key and client_id in double quotes and put them on a single line. For reference, here's what my credentials file looks like (with some omitted private pieces replaced with three periods—...).

```
ios:
  # ...

fcm:
  type: service_account
  project_id: hiking-journal-...
  private_key_id: 76f1f1...
  private_key: "-----BEGIN PRIVATE KEY-----\nMIIEvQIBADANBgkqhkiG9w0BAQ..."
  client_email: firebase-adminsdk-...@hiking-journal.gserviceaccount.com
  client_id: "11700..."
  auth_uri: https://accounts.google.com/o/oauth2/auth
  token_uri: https://oauth2.googleapis.com/token
  auth_provider_x509_cert_url: https://www.googleapis.com/oauth2/v1/certs
  client_x509_cert_url: https://www.googleapis.com/robot/...
  universe_domain: googleapis.com
```

We now have everything we need on the Rails server to send both iOS and Android notifications. Next, we'll connect our Android app to the Firebase project and add the dependencies needed to receive notifications.

Add FCM Dependencies

Back in the Firebase Console, click the General tab at the top and scroll down. Click the google-services.json link to download the JSON file to your machine. Copy it over to android/app.

Our Firebase project is now connected with our Android app. Next up is configuring the Android app to receive notifications.

Open Android Studio and add the Google Services plugin and Firebase dependencies to the app's build.gradle.kts.

```
ch10_51/android/app/build.gradle.kts
plugins {
    alias(libs.plugins.android.application)
    alias(libs.plugins.kotlin.android)
    alias(libs.plugins.compose.compiler)
    id("com.google.android.libraries.mapsplatform.secrets-gradle-plugin")
    id("org.jetbrains.kotlin.plugin.serialization")
    id("com.google.gms.google-services")
}

// ...

dependencies {
    // ...
    implementation("androidx.compose.ui:ui-tooling-preview")
    implementation("com.google.maps.android:maps-compose:6.1.0")
    implementation("org.jetbrains.kotlinx:kotlinx-serialization-json:1.8.1")
    implementation(platform("com.google.firebase:firebase-bom:33.12.0"))
    implementation("com.google.firebase:firebase-messaging")
    debugImplementation("androidx.compose.ui:ui-tooling")
    testImplementation(libs.junit)
    androidTestImplementation(libs.androidx.junit)
    androidTestImplementation(libs.androidx.espresso.core)
}
```

Then, add the Google Services plugin to the module's build.gradle.kts.

```
ch10_51/android/build.gradle.kts
// Top-level build file where you can add configuration options common to all
// sub-projects/modules.
plugins {
    alias(libs.plugins.android.application) apply false
    alias(libs.plugins.kotlin.android) apply false
    alias(libs.plugins.compose.compiler) apply false
    id("org.jetbrains.kotlin.plugin.serialization") version "2.0.0" apply false
➤   id("com.google.gms.google-services") version "4.4.2" apply false
}

buildscript {
    dependencies {
        classpath(
            "com.google.android.libraries.mapsplatform" +
                    ".secrets-gradle-plugin:secrets-gradle-plugin:2.0.1"
        )
    }
}
```

Finally, add the notification permission to the manifest.

```
ch10_51/android/app/src/main/AndroidManifest.xml
<manifest xmlns:android="http://schemas.android.com/apk/res/android"
    xmlns:tools="http://schemas.android.com/tools">

    <uses-permission android:name="android.permission.INTERNET" />
➤   <uses-permission android:name="android.permission.POST_NOTIFICATIONS" />

    <!-- ... -->
</manifest>
```

OK, enough configuration. Sync Gradle and then let's write some Kotlin!

Authorize Sending Notifications on Android

As on iOS, we need the user's permission to send them notifications on Android. Once we receive confirmation, we'll get a token and POST it to the Rails server to associate with the user. On iOS, we had a bridge component that directly displayed the system prompt asking for such and a view model to make the network request.

We'll start on Android in the same way, with NotificationTokenComponent. Create a new file under the components package and name it NotificationTokenComponent.kt. Then, add the boilerplate code for a bridge component.

```
ch10_52/android/app/src/main/java/com/masilotti ... journal/components/NotificationTokenComponent.kt
package com.masilotti.hikingjournal.components

import dev.hotwire.core.bridge.BridgeComponent
import dev.hotwire.core.bridge.BridgeDelegate
import dev.hotwire.core.bridge.Message
```

```
import dev.hotwire.navigation.destinations.HotwireDestination

class NotificationTokenComponent(
    name: String,
    private val bridgeDelegate: BridgeDelegate<HotwireDestination>
) : BridgeComponent<HotwireDestination>(name, bridgeDelegate) {

    override fun onReceive(message: Message) {
        // Request notification permission.
    }
}
```

Unlike on iOS, requesting runtime permissions[14] must be done when *initializing* a Fragment. It can't be done dynamically as we did on iOS. So, for Android, you need an additional step: a custom HotwireWebFragment extension (subclass) to add your permission request logic.

Wait, What's a HotwireWebFragment?

A HotwireWebFragment is the base class from which all "standard" web fragments (non-dialogs) in a Hotwire app should extend from.

Every time a web-powered screen is displayed, a HotwireWebFragment is used. This fragment, provided by Hotwire Native Android, handles everything related to the web view and the content it's rendering.

By extending (subclassing) this, we can add additional functionality or logic without having to worry about the details of the managed web view.

Create a new class in the fragments package and name it WebFragment. Reuse the same @HotwireDestinationDeepLink as HotwireWebFragment to ensure every web screen gets rendered with this fragment. Remember, we set this in our path configuration in code on page 57.

ch10_53/android/app/src/main/java/com/masilotti/hikingjournal/fragments/WebFragment.kt
```
package com.masilotti.hikingjournal.fragments

import dev.hotwire.navigation.destinations.HotwireDestinationDeepLink
import dev.hotwire.navigation.fragments.HotwireWebFragment

@HotwireDestinationDeepLink("hotwire://fragment/web")
class WebFragment : HotwireWebFragment() {
}
```

Add a private requestPermissionLauncher property that, when granted, calls registerForTokenChanges(). We'll launch this dynamically from the bridge component.

---

14. https://developer.android.com/training/permissions/requesting#request-permission

ch10_54/android/app/src/main/java/com/masilotti/hikingjournal/fragments/WebFragment.kt
```kotlin
package com.masilotti.hikingjournal.fragments

import androidx.activity.result.contract.ActivityResultContracts
import dev.hotwire.navigation.destinations.HotwireDestinationDeepLink
import dev.hotwire.navigation.fragments.HotwireWebFragment

@HotwireDestinationDeepLink("hotwire://fragment/web")
class WebFragment : HotwireWebFragment() {
    private val contract = ActivityResultContracts.RequestPermission()
    private val requestPermissionLauncher =
        registerForActivityResult(contract) { isGranted ->
            if (isGranted) registerForTokenChanges()
        }

    private fun registerForTokenChanges() {
    }
}
```

Inside of registerForTokenChanges(), add a completion handler to the Firebase token. Every time the value of the token changes, this code will be called. After we create the view model, we'll come back and replace the comment to make the network request.

ch10_55/android/app/src/main/java/com/masilotti/hikingjournal/fragments/WebFragment.kt
```kotlin
package com.masilotti.hikingjournal.fragments

import androidx.activity.result.contract.ActivityResultContracts
import com.google.firebase.messaging.FirebaseMessaging
import dev.hotwire.navigation.destinations.HotwireDestinationDeepLink
import dev.hotwire.navigation.fragments.HotwireWebFragment

@HotwireDestinationDeepLink("hotwire://fragment/web")
class WebFragment : HotwireWebFragment() {
    private val contract = ActivityResultContracts.RequestPermission()
    private val requestPermissionLauncher =
        registerForActivityResult(contract) { isGranted ->
            if (isGranted) registerForTokenChanges()
        }

    private fun registerForTokenChanges() {
        val firebase = FirebaseMessaging.getInstance()
        firebase.token.addOnCompleteListener { task ->
            if (task.isSuccessful) {
                // POST token to server.
            }
        }
    }
}
```

Wrap up WebFragment by creating a public function to launch the requestPermissionLauncher. Make sure to check for the device's SDK version, too. Before

Tiramasu (Android 13), developers didn't need to ask permission to send notifications.

ch10_56/android/app/src/main/java/com/masilotti/hikingjournal/fragments/WebFragment.kt

```
package com.masilotti.hikingjournal.fragments

import android.Manifest
import android.os.Build
import androidx.activity.result.contract.ActivityResultContracts
import com.google.firebase.messaging.FirebaseMessaging
import dev.hotwire.navigation.destinations.HotwireDestinationDeepLink
import dev.hotwire.navigation.fragments.HotwireWebFragment

@HotwireDestinationDeepLink("hotwire://fragment/web")
class WebFragment : HotwireWebFragment() {
    // ...

    fun requestNotificationPermission() {
        if (Build.VERSION.SDK_INT >= Build.VERSION_CODES.TIRAMISU) {
            val permission = Manifest.permission.POST_NOTIFICATIONS
            requestPermissionLauncher.launch(permission)
        }
    }

    private fun registerForTokenChanges() {
        // ...
    }
}
```

Back in NotificationTokenComponent, cast the bridgeDelegate.destination as a WebFragment, our custom subclass, just as we did in the ButtonComponent code on page 153.

ch10_57/android/app/src/main/java/com/masilotti ... journal/components/NotificationTokenComponent.kt

```
package com.masilotti.hikingjournal.components

import com.masilotti.hikingjournal.fragments.WebFragment
import dev.hotwire.core.bridge.BridgeComponent
import dev.hotwire.core.bridge.BridgeDelegate
import dev.hotwire.core.bridge.Message
import dev.hotwire.navigation.destinations.HotwireDestination

class NotificationTokenComponent(
    name: String,
    private val bridgeDelegate: BridgeDelegate<HotwireDestination>
) : BridgeComponent<HotwireDestination>(name, bridgeDelegate) {
    private val fragment: WebFragment
        get() = bridgeDelegate.destination.fragment as WebFragment

    override fun onReceive(message: Message) {
        fragment.requestNotificationPermission()
    }
}
```

Can you guess what's next? I'll give you a hint: we just created a new bridge component and a new fragment. That's right! We need to register these with Hotwire Native.

Open HikingJournalApplication and register them with the framework. While you're in there, make sure to initialize Firebase, too.

```
ch10_58/android/app/src/main/java/com/masilotti/hikingjournal/HikingJournalApplication.kt
package com.masilotti.hikingjournal

import android.app.Application
➤ import com.google.firebase.FirebaseApp
import com.masilotti.hikingjournal.activities.baseURL
import com.masilotti.hikingjournal.components.ButtonComponent
➤ import com.masilotti.hikingjournal.components.NotificationTokenComponent
import com.masilotti.hikingjournal.fragments.MapFragment
➤ import com.masilotti.hikingjournal.fragments.WebFragment
import dev.hotwire.core.bridge.BridgeComponentFactory
import dev.hotwire.core.bridge.KotlinXJsonConverter
import dev.hotwire.core.config.Hotwire
// ...

class HikingJournalApplication : Application() {
    override fun onCreate() {
        super.onCreate()

➤       FirebaseApp.initializeApp(this)

        Hotwire.loadPathConfiguration(
            // ...
        )

        Hotwire.registerFragmentDestinations(
            MapFragment::class,
➤           WebFragment::class,
        )

        Hotwire.registerBridgeComponents(
            BridgeComponentFactory("button", ::ButtonComponent),
➤           BridgeComponentFactory(
➤               "notification-token",
➤               ::NotificationTokenComponent
➤           )
        )

        Hotwire.config.jsonConverter = KotlinXJsonConverter()
    }
}
```

We're now requesting permission from the user and gathering the notification token. All that's left is to get the token to the server.

POST Firebase Token to Server

We'll POST the notification token to the server with a view model. Create a new file under the viewmodels package and name it NotificationTokenViewModel. Add a public function that accepts a String.

ch10_59/android/app/src/main/java/com/masilotti … journal/viewmodels/NotificationTokenViewModel.kt

```
package com.masilotti.hikingjournal.viewmodels

import kotlinx.coroutines.Dispatchers
import kotlinx.coroutines.withContext

class NotificationTokenViewModel {
    suspend fun registerToken(token: String) = withContext(Dispatchers.IO) {
    }
}
```

The withContext(Dispatchers.IO) at the end of this function lets it run on a background thread—perfect for making network requests. It will also leave our implementation a bit cleaner since we won't have to nest a withContext() block.

Next, create a URL and open a connection on it. Cast this result to a HttpURLConnection so we can set the HTTP method and grab the response code. Make sure to identify the request as JSON so our server can parse the payload correctly.

ch10_60/android/app/src/main/java/com/masilotti … journal/viewmodels/NotificationTokenViewModel.kt

```
package com.masilotti.hikingjournal.viewmodels

➤ import com.masilotti.hikingjournal.activities.baseURL
  import kotlinx.coroutines.Dispatchers
  import kotlinx.coroutines.withContext
➤ import java.net.HttpURLConnection
➤ import java.net.URL

  class NotificationTokenViewModel {
      suspend fun registerToken(token: String) = withContext(Dispatchers.IO) {
➤         val url = URL("$baseURL/notification_tokens")
➤
➤         val connection = url.openConnection() as HttpURLConnection
➤         connection.requestMethod = "POST"
➤         connection.setRequestProperty("Content-Type", "application/json")
      }
  }
```

The /notification_tokens endpoint authorizes the user with the web-based cookie via current_user. On iOS, the cookies are copied over for us automatically. On Android, we need to do this ourselves for every native HTTP request.

ch10_61/android/app/src/main/java/com/masilotti … journal/viewmodels/NotificationTokenViewModel.kt

```
package com.masilotti.hikingjournal.viewmodels

➤ import android.webkit.CookieManager
```

```
import com.masilotti.hikingjournal.activities.baseURL
import kotlinx.coroutines.Dispatchers
import kotlinx.coroutines.withContext
import java.net.HttpURLConnection
import java.net.URL

class NotificationTokenViewModel {
    suspend fun registerToken(token: String) = withContext(Dispatchers.IO) {
        val url = URL("$baseURL/notification_tokens")

        val connection = url.openConnection() as HttpURLConnection
        connection.requestMethod = "POST"
        connection.setRequestProperty("Content-Type", "application/json")

        CookieManager.getInstance().getCookie(baseURL)?.let {
            connection.setRequestProperty("Cookie", it)
        }
    }
}
```

Next, add the notification token payload as JSON to the request.

ch10_62/android/app/src/main/java/com/masilotti ... journal/viewmodels/NotificationTokenViewModel.kt

```
package com.masilotti.hikingjournal.viewmodels

import android.webkit.CookieManager
import com.masilotti.hikingjournal.activities.baseURL
import kotlinx.coroutines.Dispatchers
import kotlinx.coroutines.withContext
import org.json.JSONObject
import java.io.OutputStreamWriter
import java.net.HttpURLConnection
import java.net.URL

class NotificationTokenViewModel {
    suspend fun registerToken(token: String) = withContext(Dispatchers.IO) {
        // ...

        CookieManager.getInstance().getCookie(baseURL)?.let {
            connection.setRequestProperty("Cookie", it)
        }

        val body = JSONObject().apply {
            put("token", token)
            put("platform", "FCM")
        }
        OutputStreamWriter(connection.outputStream).use { writer ->
            writer.write(body.toString())
        }
    }
}
```

Trigger the connection by referencing the status code. In an ideal world, we'd check this value to make sure the request succeeded, but that's out of this book's scope. For now, all we care about is exceptions.

ch10_63/android/app/src/main/java/com/masilotti ... journal/viewmodels/NotificationTokenViewModel.kt

```
// ...

class NotificationTokenViewModel {
    suspend fun registerToken(token: String) = withContext(Dispatchers.IO) {
        // ...

        OutputStreamWriter(connection.outputStream).use { writer ->
            writer.write(body.toString())
        }

        connection.responseCode
    }
}
```

Wrap the entire function implementation in a try/catch block to catch any exceptions raised when making the network request.

ch10_64/android/app/src/main/java/com/masilotti ... journal/viewmodels/NotificationTokenViewModel.kt

```
// ...

class NotificationTokenViewModel {
    suspend fun registerToken(token: String) = withContext(Dispatchers.IO) {
        try {
            val url = URL("$baseURL/notification_tokens")
            // ...

            connection.responseCode
        } catch (e: Exception) {
            e.printStackTrace()
        }
    }
}
```

Finally, back in WebFragment, call viewModel.registerToken() in the token change handler. Wrapping this call in a launched lifecycleScope ensures it occurs on a background thread.

ch10_65/android/app/src/main/java/com/masilotti/hikingjournal/fragments/WebFragment.kt

```
package com.masilotti.hikingjournal.fragments

import android.Manifest
import android.os.Build
import androidx.activity.result.contract.ActivityResultContracts
import androidx.lifecycle.lifecycleScope
import com.google.firebase.messaging.FirebaseMessaging
import com.masilotti.hikingjournal.viewmodels.NotificationTokenViewModel
import dev.hotwire.navigation.destinations.HotwireDestinationDeepLink
import dev.hotwire.navigation.fragments.HotwireWebFragment
```

```
import kotlinx.coroutines.launch

@HotwireDestinationDeepLink("hotwire://fragment/web")
class WebFragment : HotwireWebFragment() {
    private val viewModel = NotificationTokenViewModel()
    // ...

    private fun registerForTokenChanges() {
        val firebase = FirebaseMessaging.getInstance()
        firebase.token.addOnCompleteListener { task ->
            if (task.isSuccessful) {
                viewLifecycleOwner.lifecycleScope.launch {
                    viewModel.registerToken(task.result)
                }
            }
        }
    }
}
```

Everything is now in place to register an FCM token and receive notifications. Let's see it in action.

Run the app and sign in. Then, put the app in the background by pressing the circle button to the right of the emulator.

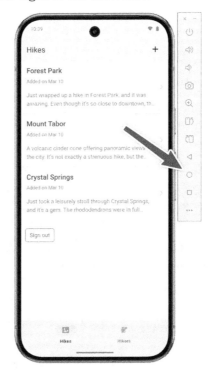

In your machine's browser, navigate to the Forest Park hike and click the heart to unlike the hike, then again to re-like it. You'll see a tiny circle up in the status bar indicating a successful push notification.

Click and drag down from that area to open the notification drawer to view the full notification.

Our Android app can now register for and receive push notifications from our Rails server. All that's left is to handle what happens when the notification is tapped.

Route Android Notifications

We'll route the `path` from the notification payload, just as on iOS.

On Android, every notification provides a custom `Intent` to the app's main activity. Open `MainActivity` and pass the `Intent` to a new private function named `handleDeepLink(intent: Intent?)`.

Android Intents are like Rails controller actions combined with `redirect_to`. They're how Android apps launch activities or services and pass data between them. Think of them as structured messages that tell the system what you want to do (like open a screen or share content) and what data to include.

ch10_66/android/app/src/main/java/com/masilotti/hikingjournal/activities/MainActivity.kt

```
package com.masilotti.hikingjournal.activities

import android.content.Intent
import android.os.Bundle
import android.view.View
import androidx.activity.enableEdgeToEdge
// ...

class MainActivity : HotwireActivity() {
    // ...
```

```
    private fun initializeBottomTabs() {
        // ...
    }

➤   override fun onStart() {
➤       super.onStart()
➤
➤       handleDeepLink(intent)
➤   }
➤   private fun handleDeepLink(intent: Intent?) {
➤   }
    }
```

Extract the path as a String and build a URL via baseURL. Then pass this to the current Navigator. Wrap up the function by setting the Intent to null, to make sure we don't route the same notification again on the next app launch.

ch10_67/android/app/src/main/java/com/masilotti/hikingjournal/activities/MainActivity.kt
```
// ...

class MainActivity : HotwireActivity() {
    // ...

    private fun handleDeepLink(intent: Intent?) {
➤       val path = intent?.getStringExtra("path")
➤       path?.let {
➤           delegate.currentNavigator?.route("$baseURL$it")
➤       }
➤       this.intent = null
    }
}
```

This function will be called every time the app launches, even when there isn't a notification to route. That's why we need to make sure there is a path extra in the Intent with the optional unwrapping.

Run the app, background it, and trigger another notification. This time, tap the notification. The app will route the hike page, just as on iOS, as shown in the screenshot on page 238. Excellent! You've achieved feature parity with iOS once again.

Recapping Push Notifications

You just learned how to implement push notifications across both mobile platforms.

On the clients, you kicked off the authorization request from a bridge component that's triggered when the user signs in. Then, when accepted, the notification token is POSTed to the server via a view model. Finally,

when the notification was tapped, you built a URL from the path and deep linked to it via a Navigator.

On the Rails side, you learned how to set up Noticed to send notifications via APNs and FCM. You created a Notifier subclass to contain all of your notification logic, like only sending notifications to registered devices and embedding the path in the payload. And you're keeping your authorization tokens secure by storing them in Rails credentials.

With this scaffolding in place, you can further improve your notifications, *all from the server.* You could add a second line of text via subtitle on iOS[15] and body on Android.[16] Let's say you add the ability to comment on hikes. Create a NewCommentNotifier and start sending notifications—no additional client code needed. Even deep linking to a new path will work.

What's Next?

Congratulations, you've completed *Hotwire Native for Rails Developers*!

You now know how to build iOS and Android apps powered by your Rails server. You understand the Hotwire Native mindset of leaving as much logic as possible on the server. And you know how to progressively enhance the app with bridge components and fully native screens. You are well on your

---

15. https://developer.apple.com/documentation/usernotifications/generating-a-remote-notification
16. https://firebase.google.com/docs/cloud-messaging/concept-options

way to creating sustainable, low-maintenance mobile apps that your users will love.

The beauty of the techniques you've learned is that you can apply them to *any* native API. Need some data from HealthKit?[17] Build a new bridge component and grab the data in onReceive(message:). What about a fully native home screen? Follow the steps from Chapter 5, Render Native Screens with SwiftUI, on page 81, and Chapter 6, Render Native Screens with Jetpack Compose, on page 103, replacing everything related to a map with your domain.

If you're looking for inspiration on what to build next, check out the Hotwire Native directory,[18] a community-run website listing apps available for download in the app stores. Some are even open source. For more details on iOS and Android development, Apple's iOS Developer Documentation[19] and Google's Android Developer Guides[20] are great places to go deeper with native capabilities.

To stay up-to-date on the latest Hotwire Native releases and techniques, visit my website at masilotti.com.[21] I post weekly-ish, covering tips and techniques for efficiently building mobile apps with ease. I also share some behind-the-scenes previews of what I'm currently working on.

Finally, if you need help with *your* app, please don't hesitate to reach out. I've helped dozens of businesses launch their Hotwire Native apps and consulted for twice as many. I can do the coding myself, advise as your team builds, or level up your developers with private training. Send me an email at joe@masilotti.com; I'd love to hear from you!

---

17. https://developer.apple.com/documentation/healthkit
18. https://hotwirenative.directory
19. https://developer.apple.com/documentation/
20. https://developer.android.com/docs
21. https://masilotti.com/

Index

Thank you!

We hope you enjoyed this book and that you're already thinking about what you want to learn next. To help make that decision easier, we're offering you this gift.

Head on over to https://pragprog.com right now, and use the coupon code BUYANOTHER2025 to save 30% on your next ebook. Offer is void where prohibited or restricted. This offer does not apply to any edition of *The Pragmatic Programmer* ebook.

And if you'd like to share your own expertise with the world, why not propose a writing idea to us? After all, many of our best authors started off as our readers, just like you. With up to a 50% royalty, world-class editorial services, and a name you trust, there's nothing to lose. Visit https://pragprog.com/become-an-author/ today to learn more and to get started.

Thank you for your continued support. We hope to hear from you again soon!

The Pragmatic Bookshelf

Agile Web Development with Rails 8

The eighth major release of Rails focuses on the ability to produce production-ready applications. It achieves this while building upon and retaining the ability to produce fantastic user experiences, and achieves all the benefits of single-page applications at a fraction of the complexity. Rails 8 introduces Kamal 2, Thruster, new database adapters, replaces the asset pipeline, and adds a new authentication generator. The result is a toolkit so powerful that it allows a single individual to create modern applications upon which they can build a competitive business—the way it used to be.

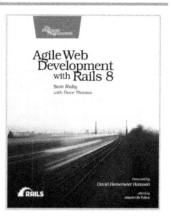

Sam Ruby
(488 pages) ISBN: 9798888651346. $67.95
https://pragprog.com/book/rails8

Rails Scales!

Rails doesn't scale. So say the naysayers. They're wrong. Ruby on Rails runs some of the biggest sites in the world, impacting the lives of millions of users while efficiently crunching petabytes of data. This book reveals how they do it, and how you can apply the same techniques to your applications. Optimize everything necessary to make an application function at scale: monitoring, product design, Ruby code, software architecture, database access, caching, and more. Even if your app may never have millions of users, you reduce the costs of hosting and maintaining it.

Cristian Planas
(270 pages) ISBN: 9798888651025. $52.95
https://pragprog.com/book/cprpo

High Performance PostgreSQL for Rails

Build faster, more reliable Rails apps by taking the best advanced PostgreSQL and Active Record capabilities, and using them to solve your application scale and growth challenges. Gain the skills needed to comfortably work with multi-terabyte databases, and with complex Active Record, SQL, and specialized Indexes. Develop your skills with PostgreSQL on your laptop, then take them into production, while keeping everything in sync. Make slow queries fast, perform any schema or data migration without errors, use scaling techniques like read/write splitting, partitioning, and sharding, to meet demanding workload requirements from Internet scale consumer apps to enterprise SaaS.

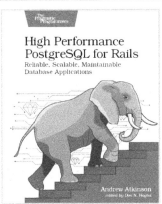

Andrew Atkinson
(454 pages) ISBN: 9798888650387. $64.95
https://pragprog.com/book/aapsql

Programming Ruby 1.9 & 2.0 (4th edition)

Ruby is the fastest growing and most exciting dynamic language out there. If you need to get working programs delivered fast, you should add Ruby to your toolbox.

This book is the only complete reference for both Ruby 1.9 and Ruby 2.0, the very latest version of Ruby.

Dave Thomas, with Chad Fowler and Andy Hunt
(886 pages) ISBN: 9781937785499. $50
https://pragprog.com/book/ruby4

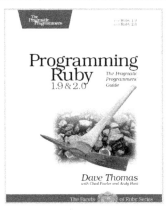

Next-Level A/B Testing

The better the tools you have in your experimentation toolkit, the better off teams will be shipping and evaluating new features on a product. Learn how to create robust A/B testing strategies that evolve with your product and engineering needs. See how to run experiments quickly, efficiently, and at less cost with the overarching goal of improving your product experience and your company's bottom line.

Leemay Nassery
(226 pages) ISBN: 9798888651308. $53.95
https://pragprog.com/book/abtestprac

Practical A/B Testing

Whether you're a catalyst for organizational change or have the support you need to create an engineering culture that embraces A/B testing, this book will help you do it right. The step-by-step instructions will demystify the entire process, from constructing an A/B test to breaking down the decision factors to build an engineering platform. When you're ready to run the A/B test of your dreams, you'll have the perfect blueprint.

Leemay Nassery
(166 pages) ISBN: 9798888650080. $29.95
https://pragprog.com/book/abtest

The Pragmatic Bookshelf

The Pragmatic Bookshelf features books written by professional developers for professional developers. The titles continue the well-known Pragmatic Programmer style and continue to garner awards and rave reviews. As development gets more and more difficult, the Pragmatic Programmers will be there with more titles and products to help you stay on top of your game.

Visit Us Online

This Book's Home Page
https://pragprog.com/book/jmnative
Source code from this book, errata, and other resources. Come give us feedback, too!

Keep Up-to-Date
https://pragprog.com
Join our announcement mailing list (low volume) or follow us on Twitter @pragprog for new titles, sales, coupons, hot tips, and more.

New and Noteworthy
https://pragprog.com/news
Check out the latest Pragmatic developments, new titles, and other offerings.

Save on the ebook

Save on the ebook versions of this title. Owning the paper version of this book entitles you to purchase the electronic versions at a terrific discount.

PDFs are great for carrying around on your laptop—they are hyperlinked, have color, and are fully searchable. Most titles are also available for the iPhone and iPod touch, Amazon Kindle, and other popular e-book readers.

Send a copy of your receipt to support@pragprog.com and we'll provide you with a discount coupon.

Contact Us

Online Orders:	*https://pragprog.com/catalog*
Customer Service:	*support@pragprog.com*
International Rights:	*translations@pragprog.com*
Academic Use:	*academic@pragprog.com*
Write for Us:	*http://write-for-us.pragprog.com*

www.ingramcontent.com/pod-product-compliance
Lightning Source LLC
LaVergne TN
LVHW081338050326
832903LV00024B/1197